"Now I Get It!"

12 Ten-Minute Classroom Drama Skits for Science, Math, Language, and Social Studies

Volume I
for Grades K–3

by L.E. McCullough, Ph.D.

FOCUSED LEARNING EXERCISES
TO BOOST COMPREHENSION AND CREATIVITY
IN THE ELEMENTARY CLASSROOM

YOUNG ACTORS SERIES

A Smith and Kraus Book

A Smith and Kraus Book
Published by Smith and Kraus, Inc.
177 Lyme Road, Hanover, NH 03755

First Edition: September 2000
10 9 8 7 6 5 4 3 2 1

Cover and Text Design by Julia Hill Gignoux, Freedom Hill Design
Cover photo by L.E. McCullough: Students at the Key Learning
Community (Indianapolis Public School #2) prepare a presentation in
Ms. Tina Nehrling's class.

The Library of Congress Cataloging-In-Publication Data
McCullough, L.E.
Now I get it! : 12 ten-minute classroom drama skits for science, math,
language, and social studies / by L.E. McCullough. —1st ed.
p. cm. — (Young actors series)
"Focused learning exercises to boost comprehension and creativity
in the elementary classroom."
Contents: v.1. For grades K–3 — v.2. For grades 4–6.
ISBN 1-57525-161-2 (vol.1) — ISBN 1-57525-162-0 (vol.2)
1. Children's plays, American. 2. Drama in education.
I. Title. II. Young actor series.
PS3563.C35297 N69 2000
812'.54—dc21   00-058778

This book is dedicated to all my teachers throughout my life, beginning with my parents, Ervin and Isabel McCullough. Looking back, I wish I knew then what I know now but didn't have a clue I'd ever need to know. (Guess that's what teachers are for. . .)

CONTENTS

Foreword vi

Language Arts:

The Parts of Speech (Syntax) 2
"May I Quote That?" (Writing) 18
Antonym — Synonym (Vocabulary) 28

Mathematics:

Even and Odd Numbers (Math) 40
Lines and Shapes (Geometry) 51

Science:

Fossils (Life Science) 62
Vitamins (Human Body) 70
The Planets (Earth Science) 79

Social Studies:

Home Sweet Biome (Geography) 90
A Child's Day in Rural America, 1876 (History) 105
What a Government Does (Citizenship) 121
"Get Me Information, Please!" (Current Events) 130

Foreword

Education is a social process. Education is growth. Education is not preparation for life. Education is life itself.
John Dewey, Educator

Good teaching is one-fourth preparation and three-fourths theatre.
Gail Godwin, Author

The greatest sign of success for a teacher is to be able to say, "The children are now working as if I did not exist."
Maria Montessori, Educator

One of the most profound concepts to have emerged in educational philosophy during the last decade is the realization that people have different, equally valid ways of learning. Based on their own unique experiences, frames of reference, prior knowledge and cognitive skills and structures, different individuals possess different "intelligences" and will understand and utilize information differently.

Some people learn more easily by visual reference, others by focusing on auditory cues. Some learn best by reading and rote memorization, others by hands-on doing and problem-solving tasks. It has become clear that, along the daily journey of acquiring knowledge, there are many paths to the same goal.

The challenge for today's educator — at any grade level — is to create an interactive and collaborative learning environment that can accommodate students' varying "intelligences." Drama, with its inherent capacity to tap and synthesize a wide range of skills and expressive modes, is a highly effective way of achieving this goal.

The plays in the "*Now* I Get It!" series are short drama pieces designed to help teachers convey basic curriculum material in Science, Math, Language and Social Studies. While almost any play can be used in some way to complement or illustrate a particular topic at hand, the "*Now* I Get It!" plays are specifically designed to serve as focused learning exercises to boost comprehension and creativity in the elementary classroom.

I've called these plays *skits,* not to downgrade their utility or seriousness of purpose but rather to reassure teachers that one need not be a trained drama specialist to make effective use of basic theatrical techniques in the classroom. There are several dictionary definitions of *skit*; the one I prefer is "a short dramatic piece, especially one done by amateurs,"[1] possibly derived from an 18th-century English dialect term *skite*, meaning "to move quickly" — which is exactly what a well-written, well-executed skit does.

As an aid to curriculum development during the last decade, many state education departments have adopted basic standards or "proficiencies" in each subject area. These proficiencies are goals for student learning that emphasize specific concepts and skills; teachers are free to organize methods of instruction to best meet their students' needs.

In the State of Indiana, where I currently reside, the Indiana Department of Education has cited the following eight proficiencies in English/Language Arts[2] :

- exhibiting a positive attitude toward language and learning
- selecting and applying effective strategies for reading
- comprehending developmentally appropriate materials
- select and using developmentally appropriate strategies for writing

- writing for different purposes and audiences producing a variety of forms
- using prior knowledge and content area information to make critical judgments
- communicating orally with people of all ages
- recognizing the interrelatedness of language, literature and culture

In effect, each English/Language Arts course at every grade level should contribute to aiding students in attaining these proficiencies. Drama facilitates this process by being an *elastic* and *inclusive* medium that offers students a firm organizational structure along with the freedom to reshape that structure into a wholly new learning experience.

Each *"Now I Get It!"* play is accompanied by a list of suggested pre- and post-play activities and discussion questions; consider these plays foundations and stepping stones for further research and learning by your students. Though each play script is self-contained and based on actual lesson material, the format allows for additional information you might want to insert. Obviously, a short skit can cover nothing more than the basic outline of a lesson and the merest surface of a topic. I have supplied only rudimentary stage and lighting directions. Use your imagination to expand or adapt the plays for your classroom space, your student population, your curriculum needs. Then, once you've got the hang of it, have students write their own plays for other lessons!

If you're a teacher, the *"Now I Get It!"* plays are a great way of imparting basic knowledge to students, then inspiring them to discover more on their own. For parents, at-home production of the plays helps parents and children achieve a "good goal" together. Parents get to see their children at their most vibrant and creative. Children get to excel for their parents, and they become more self-motivated and self-reliant, especially in terms of socializing with other children. By going through the process of creating and interpreting a play for an audience — even if the audience is only the family or the classroom — adults and children learn to listen to each other better.

And for kids, is there really any better way to learn the rules of grammar than by playing a dancing participle?

L.E. McCullough, Ph.D.
Humanities Theatre Group
Indiana University-Purdue University at Indianapolis
Indianapolis, Indiana

---

[1] *Merriam Webster's Collegiate Dictionary*, 10th Edition, 1993.
[2] *English/Language Arts Proficiency Guide: Essential Skills for Indiana Students*, Indiana Department of Education, 1999.

Acknowledgments

Terry Porter, Agape Productions; Julie Pratt McQuiston, *Arts Indiana*; Anne Laker, POLIS Center at Indiana University-Purdue University at Indianapolis; Administrative Service Center, Washington Township Schools, Indianapolis; Curriculum and Instruction Division, Indianapolis Public Schools; Jane Hughes Gignoux; J.J. Stenzoski and Rush Yelverton of the Downtown Kiwanis Club; Alan Cloe, WFYI-TV; Maureen Dobie of NUVO Newsweekly; Susan Cross, Woodward High School, Cincinnati; Debra, Ryan, and Michael Kelleher; Miss Jeanne Grubb, my father's first piano teacher, now 96 years young.

language arts

THE PARTS OF SPEECH
(Syntax)

BASIC CONCEPT:

This play highlights the basic elements of *sentence construction* and *punctuation*.

PRE- OR POST-PLAY ACTIVITIES:

- Using the blackboard, have students build 5 simple sentences based on objects in the classroom and then diagram them. Start with a subject and predicate, then add an object and a modifying adjective, adverb and prepositional phrase.

- Have students write a paragraph (with at least 5 simple sentences) that describes an activity — going to the store, feeding a dog, washing the dishes, riding a bicycle, taking a trip to a museum. Diagram the sentences, then change the verbs in the sentences with new verbs and see if the new verbs have changed the sentence structure.

- Using the paragraph above, have students make a list of alternate adjectives and adverbs; then discuss how that would change the meaning of each sentence.

DISCUSSION QUESTIONS:

- Study this sentence: *Good writing holds the interest of an intelligent reader.* How many compound words can you form using the words in this sentence?

- Can you explain the difference between a *subject pronoun* and an *object pronoun*? Read a paragraph from a book and substitute pronouns for all the nouns, then substitute nouns for pronouns.

STAGE SET: any classroom

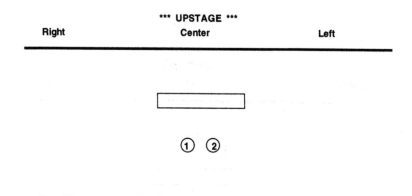

Opening Stage Plan — *The Parts of Speech*

Key:

▭ chalkboard

◯ student

1 Nora	9 Ms. Question Mark
2 Vic	10 Mr. Quotation
3 Priscilla	11 Mrs. Quotation
4 Anna	12 Connie
5 Angela	13 Clark
6 Pamela	14 Sam
7 Peter	15 Edward
8 Eric	16 Harry
	17 Patty

CAST: 17 actors, min. 8 boys (•), 9 girls (+)

+	Anna Adjective	+	Patty Parenthesis
+	Angela Adverb	•	Peter Period
+	Connie Colon	+	Pamela Preposition
•	Clark Comma	+	Priscilla Pronoun
•	Edward Ellipsis	+	Ms. Question Mark
•	Eric Exclamation Point	•	Mr. Quotation
•	Sam Semicolon	+	Mrs. Quotation
•	Harry Hyphen	•	Vic Verb
+	Nora Noun		

PROPS: chalkboard; chalk; signboards

COSTUMES: characters wear contemporary school clothes, or t-shirts and hats with their punctuation sign displayed

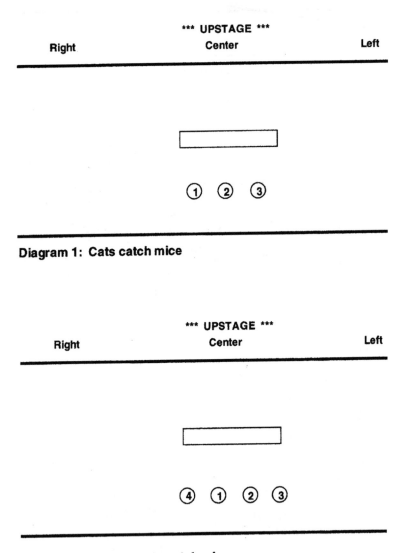

*** UPSTAGE ***

Right   Center   Left

① ② ③

Diagram 1: Cats catch mice

*** UPSTAGE ***

Right   Center   Left

④ ① ② ③

Diagram 2: Hungry cats catch mice

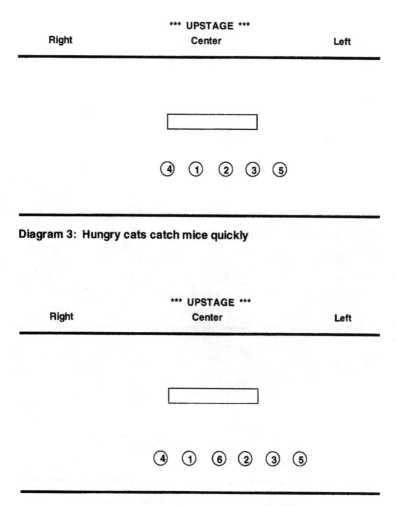

Diagram 3: Hungry cats catch mice quickly

Diagram 4: Hungry cats with sharp claws catch mice quickly

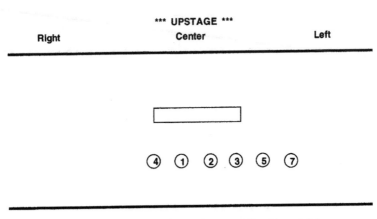

Diagram 5: Hungry cats with sharp claws catch mice quickly.

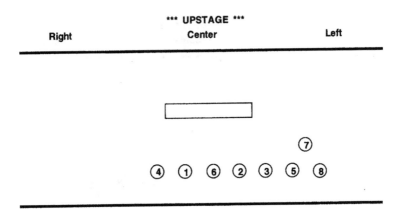

Diagram 6: Hungry cats with sharp claws catch mice quickly!

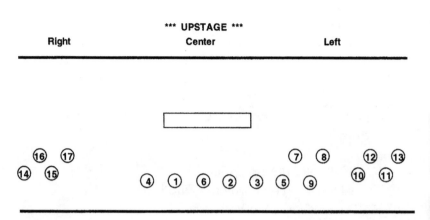

Diagram 7: Hungry cats with sharp claws catch mice quickly?

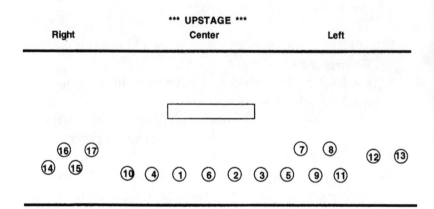

Diagram 8: "Hungry cats with sharp claws catch mice quickly?"

(LIGHTS UP FULL ON NORA NOUN at center stage. She is fumbling with several pieces of signboard, trying unsuccessfully to get them to stand up in front of the chalkboard. Finally, she drops them all on the floor.)

NORA NOUN: Oh, drat! I'll never get this to work!

(VIC VERB stands at right and observes Nora's distress.)

VIC VERB: Nora! Nora Noun!
NORA NOUN: *(peers around)* Who is it?
VIC VERB: It's me, Vic Verb.
NORA NOUN: Go away! I mean come here! I mean — oh, I don't know what I mean anymore!

(Vic crosses to center stage.)

VIC VERB: Gosh, Nora, what in the world are you doing? Wallpapering the floor?
NORA NOUN: I'm working! I have to build a whole sentence for school — by *tomorrow.*
VIC VERB: So what's the problem? People build sentences every day all over the world. The sentence is the foundation of written and spoken language.
NORA NOUN: I know what a sentence is, Vic. A sentence is a group of words stating, asking, commanding, requesting or exclaiming something. But I can't build a sentence by myself. I'm only a noun. I can be a person, place or thing — even a quality. But you need a noun and a verb to make up a sentence.
VIC VERB: Hmmm. That's true. Hey! *I'm* a verb!
NORA NOUN: Yes, you are!
VIC VERB: And I can express action, existence or occurrence.
NORA NOUN: Here, hold this.

(She picks up a signboard and hands it to him. He displays it to audience and reads the writing on front.)

VIC VERB: "Catch." Oh, that's a fun verb. A real *action* verb. Let's see your noun, Nora.

(She picks up a signboard, displays it to audience and stands to the right of Vic.)

NORA NOUN: "Cats." *(she points to his signboard and reads)* "Cats catch." That's a sentence, isn't it?

VIC VERB: It sure is. It has a noun and verb. "Cats catch." It's a perfect sentence.

NORA NOUN: But what do they catch?

VIC VERB: Huh?

NORA NOUN: I mean, isn't there something missing? "Cats catch." . . what is it they catch?

VIC VERB: Cold! They catch cold! *(laughs, stops when he sees Nora frowning)* Sorry. Bad joke.

(PRISCILLA PRONOUN enters from left.)

PRISCILLA PRONOUN: *I* can tell you.

VIC VERB: Look, it's Priscilla Pronoun.

NORA NOUN: *(turns away as Priscilla crosses haughtily to center)* Don't pay any attention to her! She's always trying to push me out of the way.

PRISCILLA PRONOUN: Hi there. Anybody need a pronoun?

NORA NOUN: And why would *we* need a pronoun?

PRISCILLA PRONOUN: Well, Nora-darling, as *you* well know, a pronoun is a word used in place of or as a substitute for a noun — like *you*. "I," "me," "you," "he," "she," "him," "her," "it," "we," "us," "they," "them" — you know, words that add a little mystery to the sentence.

VIC VERB: So you do the same thing in a sentence that a noun does?

PRISCILLA PRONOUN: Exactly. Only without being so boringly specific.

NORA NOUN: I thought you were going to tell us what cats catch?

PRISCILLA PRONOUN: Well, I guess somebody's socks are on fire! Okay, here's how it is, kitties. You know that a sentence has to have a noun and verb, right? When you diagram the sentence—

VIC VERB: Diagram? What's a diagram?

PRISCILLA PRONOUN: A diagram is like an x-ray of the sentence. It shows you how the words relate to each other, just like an x-ray shows how all the bones fit together in your body.

NORA NOUN: *(in a loud whisper)* She is *such* a know-it-all!

(Priscilla goes to chalkboard and draws a subject/predicate diagram, then "cats" catch.")

PRISCILLA PRONOUN: When you diagram a sentence, the noun is called a "subject." The verb is called a "predicate." Here's the sentence you two built: "cats catch." A noun and a verb. A subject and a predicate.

NORA NOUN: Okay, Priscilla. But where's the missing thing you promised to help us find?

VIC VERB: What missing thing?

NORA NOUN: You know, the thing, the object!

PRISCILLA PRONOUN: You're looking at her.

VIC VERB: Huh?

PRISCILLA PRONOUN: After the subject and the predicate comes "the object." The object of the sentence is a noun that directly or indirectly receives the action of a verb.

(Priscilla goes to chalkboard and adds the object space to the diagram.)

NORA NOUN: Such as?

VIC VERB: "Cats catch mice."

PRISCILLA PRONOUN: No grass growing under that boy's feet!

(Priscilla adds "mice" to diagram in object space; Vic picks up a signboard that reads "mice" and hands it to her; she stands to left of Vic, displaying signboard to audience, as they all line up facing audience — see Diagram 1.)

NORA NOUN: Cats. . .

VIC VERB: . . . catch. . .

PRISCILLA PRONOUN: . . . mice. Now we have a sentence with an object.

(ANNA ADJECTIVE and ANGELA ADVERB enter from right.)

VIC VERB: Look, it's Anna Adjective!

ANNA ADJECTIVE: Hi, guys!

NORA NOUN: And Angela Adverb!

ANGELA ADVERB: What are you doing?

VIC VERB: Building a sentence. Do you want to help?

ANNA ADJECTIVE: Sure! I'm an adjective, which means I describe things or people or places. Let's see. . .

(Anna picks up a signboard that reads "hungry" and stands to right of Nora, displaying signboard to audience — see Diagram 2.)

ANNA ADJECTIVE: Hungry. . .

NORA NOUN: . . . cats. . .

VIC VERB: . . . catch. . .

PRISCILLA PRONOUN: . . . mice.

VIC VERB: How do you diagram an adjective?

ANGELA ADVERB: I'll show you.

(Angela goes to chalkboard and diagrams "hungry," then adds an adverb line writing in "quickly"; Nora hands her a signboard that reads "quickly," and Angela stands to left of Priscilla — see Diagram 3.)

ANNA ADJECTIVE: Hungry. . .

NORA NOUN: . . . cats. . .

VIC VERB: . . . catch. . .

PRISCILLA PRONOUN: . . . mice. . .

ANGELA ADVERB: . . . quickly.

VIC VERB: What's "quickly"?

ANGELA ADVERB: It's me — an adverb. An adverb is a word that tells when, where or how the action of verb occurs. Right now I'm telling you how the cats caught the mice — quickly.

(PAMELA PREPOSITION dashes in from left, waving her arms wildly.)

PAMELA PREPOSITION : Hey, everybody! Wait up! Don't forget about me!

PRISCILLA PRONOUN: It's that preppy Pamela Preposition again. She's always sneaking into things at the last minute.

PAMELA PREPOSITION: Gosh, sorry I'm a little late. *(shakes everyone's hands)* Hi, I'm Pamela Preposition, glad to meet you. Pamela Preposition, love that dress. Pamela Preposition. . . if I were running for president, would you vote for me?

NORA NOUN: Pamela, what are you doing here?

PAMELA PREPOSITION: Gee willikers, Nora — I thought you of all people would know! I'm a preposition, which means I connect a noun or pronoun to another part of the sentence, such as a verb. A preposition is a relation word, and, boy, do I have a lot of relations: "of," "by," "for," "with," "to," "in," "around," "about," "before," "after," "outside," "between."

VIC VERB: So where do you fit in this sentence, Pamela?

(Pamela picks up a signboard that reads "with sharp claws" and stands between Nora and Vic — see Diagram 4.)

PAMELA PREPOSITION: Right here with a prepositional phrase. Show them, Angela.

(Angela diagrams the prepositional phrase "with sharp claws" on chalkboard, then returns to her place in the sentence.)

ANNA ADJECTIVE: Hungry. . .

NORA NOUN: . . . cats. . .

PAMELA PREPOSITION: . . . with sharp claws. . .

VIC VERB: . . . catch. . .

PRISCILLA PRONOUN: . . . mice. . .

ANGELA ADVERB: . . . quickly.

PAMELA PREPOSITION: Prepositions always have objects, and right now I'm a prepositional phrase.

VIC VERB: Well, that's it then! We built a sentence.

ANNA ADJECTIVE: "Hungry cats with sharp claws catch mice quickly." I think it's a lovely sentence.

PETER PERIOD: *(o.s.)* Stop! Don't anybody make another move!

(Characters freeze in place as PETER PERIOD and ERIC EXCLAMATION POINT stride onstage from right.)

ANNA ADJECTIVE: It's Peter Period and Eric Exclamation Point! What do they want with us?

(As if inspecting or looking for something amiss, Peter and Eric pace sternly in front of the characters, who remain in a row with signboards displayed toward audience.)

VIC VERB: Hey, guys! We've been helping Nora Noun build a sentence.

PETER PERIOD: You have, have you? *(laughs)*

ANGELA ADVERB: It's a great sentence, don't you think?

ERIC EXCLAMATION POINT: *(laughs)* They think it's a great sentence!

PETER PERIOD: They would. Listen, you people have a big problem.

PAMELA PREPOSITION: We do?

ERIC EXCLAMATION POINT: Yeh. . . you don't have any punctuation.

VIC VERB: Punctuation?

PETER PERIOD: Not a period, not a comma. Not a question mark, nor a semicolon. None, nada, zip, zilch.

ERIC EXCLAMATION POINT: *(shouts in Vic's face)* And you call yourselves a sentence?

PETER PERIOD: May I remind you that no sentence — I repeat — no sentence is complete without appropriate punctuation.

ERIC EXCLAMATION POINT: That's us. Punctuation is the use of standardized marks and signs to separate clauses, phrases and sentences—

NORA NOUN: In order to make their meaning better understood.

PETER PERIOD: Well, if you know all about it, how come you didn't do it?

ERIC EXCLAMATION POINT: People think they can get along without us.

PETER PERIOD: People are wrong.

(Peter picks up a signboard with a period and stands to the left of Angela — see Diagram 5.)

ERIC EXCLAMATION POINT: Sound off!

ANNA ADJECTIVE: Hungry. . .

NORA NOUN: . . . cats. . .

PAMELA PREPOSITION: . . . with sharp claws. . .

VIC VERB: . . . catch. . .

PRISCILLA PRONOUN: . . . mice. . .

ANGELA ADVERB: . . . quickly.

PETER PERIOD: Period. There's your sentence.

ERIC EXCLAMATION POINT: Now, if you want a little more emphasis, you use me, an exclamation point.

(Peter moves out of the row as Eric picks up a signboard with an exclamation point and stands to the left of Angela; characters shout their lines — see Diagram 6.)

ANNA ADJECTIVE: Hungry. . .

NORA NOUN: . . . cats. . .

PAMELA PREPOSITION: . . . with sharp claws. . .

VIC VERB: . . . catch. . .

PRISCILLA PRONOUN: . . . mice. . .

ANGELA ADVERB: . . . quickly!

ERIC EXCLAMATION POINT: Exclamation point!

VIC VERB: Well, we finally did it.

NORA NOUN: Thanks everybody. I never could have built this sentence without you.

(CONNIE COLON, CLARK COMMA, MS. QUES-TION MARK, MR. QUOTATION and MRS. QUO-TATION enter from right; SAM SEMICOLON, EDWARD ELLIPSIS, PATTY PARENTHESIS and HARRY HYPHEN enter from left and converge at center; all carry a signboard with their identity.)

CONNIE COLON, CLARK COMMA, MS. QUESTION MARK, MR. QUOTATION & MRS. QUOTATION: Hey, what about us? We belong with sentences, too!

SAM SEMICOLON: You maybe don't see us all that often. . .

EDWARD ELLIPSIS: But when you need us, you'll be glad we're there.

MS. QUESTION MARK: I'm Ms. Question Mark. Use me, and your sentence becomes a question.

(She pushes Eric Exclamation Point out of the way and stands in his place holding up her signboard — see Diagram 7.)

ANNA ADJECTIVE: Hungry. . .

NORA NOUN: . . . cats. . .

PAMELA PREPOSITION: . . . with sharp claws. . .

VIC VERB: . . . catch. . .

PRISCILLA PRONOUN: . . . mice. . .

ANGELA ADVERB: . . . quickly?

MS. QUESTION MARK: Question mark?

MR. QUOTATION: I'm Mr. Quotation.

MRS. QUOTATION: I'm Mrs. Quotation.

MR. QUOTATION: We're husband and wife, and you always see us together.

MRS. QUOTATION: We're used to enclose a direct quotation — that is, when somebody says something. *(holds up example)* Abigail said, "Hungry cats with sharp claws catch mice quickly."

(Holding up their signboards, Mr. Quotation stands to right of Anna and Mrs. Quotation stands to left of Ms. Question Mark — see Diagram 8.)

CLARK COMMA: Clark Comma here. I put a slight separation between elements of a sentence. *(holds up example)* "With sharp claws, hungry cats catch mice quickly."

PATTY PARENTHESIS: I'm Patty Parenthesis. I let you know whenever the sentence has an additional word, clause or thought intended as an explanation. *(holds up example)* "Hungry cats with (really) sharp claws catch mice quickly (and how!)."

EDWARD ELLIPSIS: I'm Edward Ellipsis, and when you want to take something out of a sentence, just drop me in — one, two, three! *(holds up example)* "Hungry cats with. . . claws catch mice quickly."

CONNIE COLON: I'm Connie Colon, a mark of punctuation used before an extended quotation, explanation, example or series. *(holds up example)* "Hungry cats with sharp claws catch mice quickly: boom, boom, boom."

SAM SEMICOLON: I'm Sam Semicolon. Use me when you want to separate two independent clauses in a sentence without using a period or comma. *(holds up example)* "Hungry cats with sharp claws catch mice quickly; then they eat them."

HARRY HYPHEN: Hey, don't forget about me! I'm Harry Hyphen, a punctuation mark used between the parts of a compound word or the syllables of a divided word. *(holds up example)* "Hungry killer-cats with sharp robot-claws catch munchkin-mice quickly."

NORA NOUN: This is terrific! Doing grammar homework isn't so bad when your friends are with you.

PATTY PARENTHESIS: Homework? I thought we were invited to a party!

HARRY HYPHEN: Hey, what gives?

VIC VERB: Well, let's have a party then! A "grammar party." We can have the kids in this classroom play grammar games with us.

CLARK COMMA: They can use us parts of speech to build sentences.

SAM SEMICOLON: And punctuate them.

ALL CHARACTERS: Yeh! Grammar party! Grammar party! Grammar party!

(All characters turn to audience.)

MS. QUESTION MARK: Let the games begin!

(LIGHTS OUT)

THE END

"MAY I QUOTE THAT?"
(Writing)

BASIC CONCEPT:

This play is a grammar exercise that highlights the use of *quotation marks* and aids in developing writing, comprehension and speaking skills.

PRE- OR POST-PLAY ACTIVITIES:

• Have students write conversations (dialogues) between two speakers that use quotation marks; students can take turns performing the speaker roles. Speakers could include: Goldilocks and Papa Bear, a snowman and the sun, Jonah and the Whale, Humpty Dumpty and Mrs. Humpty Dumpty, a cat watching a bird in a tree, Sherlock Holmes and Dr. Watson solving a mystery.

• Then, expand the conversations into a larger drama skit with a Newspaper Reporter or News Anchor describing the context of the dialogue and quoting what each speaker said, as the speakers and other students act out the dialogue.

DISCUSSION QUESTIONS:

• When writing a story, why is it important to show exactly what someone says?

• The English word *quotation* comes from the Latin word *quotare*, which originally meant "to mark the number or quantity of something." If the quotation mark symbol did not exist, what other ways could you use to show someone is speaking?

STAGE SET: a bench at mid center; a chalkboard behind bench

*** UPSTAGE ***

Right	Center	Left

①　②

Opening Stage Plan — "May I Quote That?"

Key:		
▬ bench	1 Barbara	8 Tanya
	2 Crystal	9 Trudy
	3 Ginny	10 Christie
○ student	4 Matt	11 Roger
	5 Rudy	12 Penny
	6 Dave	13 Megan
▭ chalkboard	7 Jerry	

CAST: 14 actors, min. 5 boys (•), 9 girls (+)

+	Barbara	+	Crystal
+	Ginny	•	Matt
•	Rudy	•	Dave
•	Jerry	+	Tanya
+	Trudy	+	Jasmine
•	Roger	+	Penny
+	Megan	+	Ms. Winters, Teacher

PROPS: chalkboard; chalk; signboards; black marker

COSTUMES: characters wear contemporary school clothes

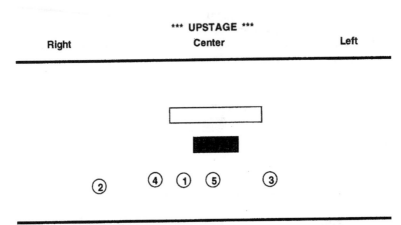

*** UPSTAGE ***

Right   Center   Left

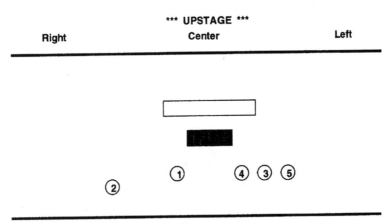

Diagram 1: "My English teacher is the best teacher in the school."

*** UPSTAGE ***

Right   Center   Left

Diagram 2: "That's really neat."

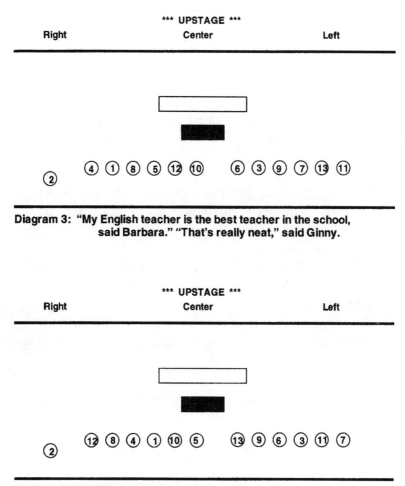

*** UPSTAGE ***

| Right | Center | Left |

④ ① ⑧ ⑤ ⑫ ⑩   ⑥ ③ ⑨ ⑦ ⑬ ⑪

②

Diagram 3: "My English teacher is the best teacher in the school, said Barbara." "That's really neat," said Ginny.

*** UPSTAGE ***

| Right | Center | Left |

⑫ ⑧ ④ ① ⑩ ⑤   ⑬ ⑨ ⑥ ③ ⑪ ⑦

②

Diagram 4: Said Barbara, "My English teacher is the best teacher in the school." Said Ginny, "That's really neat."

(LIGHTS UP FULL ON BARBARA and CRYSTAL sitting on bench at mid center.)

BARBARA: So, I said to Ginny, "My English teacher is the best teacher in the school." "That's really neat."—

CRYSTAL: Wait a minute, Barbara. Did you say "My English teacher is the best teacher in the school that's really neat."?

BARBARA: Huh?

CRYSTAL: Did you mean to say that the school is really neat? Or that your English teacher is really neat? Or that it's just really neat that your English teacher is the best teacher in the school?

BARBARA: Crystal, you're confusing me! I was telling you what I said, then what *Ginny* said about what I said.

CRYSTAL: Oh. I see.

BARBARA: Are you sure?

CRYSTAL: Well, I didn't know where the quotation marks were in what you said.

BARBARA: The what?

CRYSTAL: Has your class studied quotation marks?

BARBARA: I think so. But I might have been absent that day. Fill me in.

CRYSTAL: Well, it's pretty simple. When you write what someone speaks, you use quotation marks to set off exactly what they said.

(GINNY, MATT and RUDY enter from left and cross to center.)

BARBARA: There's Ginny now!

CRYSTAL: And Matt and Rudy are with her. Hi, guys!

GINNY, MATT & RUDY: Hi, Crystal! Hello, Barbara! What's up!

BARBARA: Crystal is telling me about quotation marks.

CRYSTAL: Let's do better than tell — let's show! Barbara, you stand here. And Matt you stand here on this side of

Barbara and Rudy over here on this side. And Ginny, stand just over here to the right of these three.

(Crystal puts Matt, then Barbara, then Rudy in a row from right to left, facing audience: Matt > Barbara > Rudy and a few feet to the left of Rudy, Ginny standing alone — see Diagram 1.)

CRYSTAL: I'll draw the quotation marks.

(Crystal takes a black marker and draws " on a signboard and " on a second signboard.)

CRYSTAL: Good. Now, we'll give Matt the first signboard with the beginning quotation mark and give Rudy the second signboard with the closing quotation mark.

(Crystal gives the signboards to Matt and Rudy who hold them up to the audience.)

CRYSTAL: Now, Barbara, say what you said to Ginny.
BARBARA: "My English teacher is the best teacher in the school."
CRYSTAL: There! That's a complete quotation. Now, Matt and Rudy, you step on either side of Ginny, while she replies:

(Matt and Rudy stand on either side of Ginny, holding their signboards up to the audience — see Diagram 2.)

GINNY: "That's really neat."
BARBARA: I see what you're talking about. Every time you write exactly what someone said, you use quotation marks to set those words off from the rest of the sentence.
CRYSTAL: Yes! Let's write it on the chalkboard!

*(Matt writes "**My English teacher is the best teacher in the school.**" on the left side of the blackboard; Rudy writes "**That's really neat.**" on the right side of chalkboard.)*

GINNY: But what do you do when you want to idenfity the two speakers who are talking? And tell which speaker said what to who?

BARBARA: We're going to need more punctuation marks for this. Look, here come Dave and Jerry!

(DAVE and JERRY enter from right.)

GINNY: And there's Trudy and Tanya!

(TRUDY and TANYA enter from left.)

CRYSTAL: We'll need more still. Here come Jasmine and Roger!

BARBARA: And Penny and Megan! Come here, guys, help us form quotations!

(JASMINE and ROGER enter from right; PENNY and MEGAN from left.)

*(Crystal distributes signboards: a " to Dave, a " to Jerry, a , to Tanya, a , to Trudy, a **said Barbara** to Penny, a **said Ginny** to Megan, a . to Jasmine, a . to Roger.)*

CRYSTAL: Okay, now everybody take your places and hold up your sign.

(From right to left facing audience stand Matt > Barbara > Tanya > Rudy > Penny > Jasmine; to the left, continuing across the stage from right to left facing audience stand Dave > Ginny > Trudy > Jerry > Megan > Roger — see Diagram 3 — with Crystal standing at down right.)

CRYSTAL: Okay. . . sound off!

MATT: Beginning quotation mark.

BARBARA: My English teacher is the best teacher in the school.

TANYA: Comma.

RUDY: Closing quotation mark.

PENNY: Said Barbara.

JASMINE: Period.

CRYSTAL: Yes! And the reply?

DAVE: Beginning quotation mark.

GINNY: That's really neat.

TRUDY: Comma.

JERRY: Closing quotation mark.

MEGAN: Said Ginny.

ROGER: Period.

CRYSTAL: Ta-dah!

(All cheer.)

ALL: Hurrah!

CRYSTAL: Wait, we're not finished. Quotations can also have the speaker at the front of the sentence. Let's write it on the chalkboard underneath the sentences above!

*(Matt writes **Said Barbara, "My English teacher is the best teacher in the school."** on the left side of the blackboard; Rudy writes **Said Ginny, "That's really neat."** on the right side of chalkboard.)*

CRYSTAL: Okay, now switch places!

(From right to left facing audience stand Penny > Tanya > Matt > Barbara > Jasmine > Rudy; to the left, continuing across the stage from right to left facing audience stand Megan > Trudy > Dave > Ginny > Roger > Jerry — see Diagram 4 — with Crystal standing at down right.)

CRYSTAL: Sound off!

PENNY: Said Barbara.

TANYA: Comma.

MATT: Beginning quotation mark.

BARBARA: My English teacher is the best teacher in the school.

JASMINE: Period.

RUDY: Closing quotation mark.

MEGAN: Said Ginny.

TRUDY: Comma.

DAVE: Beginning quotation mark.

GINNY: That's really neat.

ROGER: Period.

JERRY: Closing quotation mark.

CRYSTAL: Success!

(All cheer.)

ALL: Hurrah!

(MS. WINTERS, the teacher, enters from left.)

ALL: Good morning, Ms. Winters!

MS. WINTERS: You've done an excellent job reviewing the lesson on quotation marks. Who can tell the main rules?

MATT: Put quotation marks before and after the exact words of the speaker.

TANYA: Put a comma between the exact words of the speaker and the rest of the sentence.

BARBARA: Always start a direct quotation with a capital letter.

ROGER: Always put the ending punctuation mark of a sentence before the last quotation mark.

MS. WINTERS: That's correct! Anything else?

CRYSTAL: Always say good things about your English teacher?

MS. WINTERS: Only if you want to be quoted!

(All laugh; LIGHTS OUT.)

THE END

ANTONYM — SYNONYM
(Vocabulary)

BASIC CONCEPT:

This play is a vocabulary-building exercise using *antonyms* and *synonyms* and aids in developing reading and critical thinking skills.

PRE- OR POST-PLAY ACTIVITIES:

• Students can design crossword puzzles using antonyms and synonyms and compete via teams in solving them.

• Students can write a short story (1–2 paragraphs) and list antonyms for key words; then students act out the two versions of the story.

DISCUSSION QUESTIONS:

• Taking the examples in the Synonyms Game, have students explain what the incorrect choices mean and what the sentence would mean if they were used. (Example: "It rains very *often* in the spring." *Frequently* is the synonym for *often*; what would the sentence mean if *lightly* and *quickly* were used?)

• Take a short poem and find antonyms for 5 words. Read the new poem aloud; how do the antonyms change the meaning of the poem?

STAGE SET: 7 chairs and chalkboard at mid center

CAST: 8 actors, min. 3 boys (•), 5 girls (+)

+ Amy   + Najia
• Jeffrey   • Pedro
+ Sally   + Myrna
• Bryce   + Ms. Ballantine, Teacher

PROPS: chalkboard; chalk; signboards

COSTUMES: characters wear contemporary school clothes

(LIGHTS UP FULL ON AMY and NAJIA sitting on chairs at mid center, reading. JEFFREY enters from right and crosses to them; he addresses Amy.)

JEFFREY: Goodbye, Amy, that dress is very ugly. Would you hate to be enemies? We can leave outside. The library is noisy and warm.

AMY: *(totally astonished)* What? Najia, who is this whacko? Is he out of his mind?

NAJIA: That's Jeffrey. His nickname is "Antonym Man." He talks to people in *antonyms.*

AMY: Antonyms?

NAJIA: Antonyms are words that mean the opposite from each other.

AMY: Like "big" and "small"?

NAJIA: "Tall" and "short."

AMY: Those are antonyms.

NAJIA: Yes, they are.

JEFFREY: Goodbye, Amy, that dress is very ugly. Would you hate to be enemies? We can leave outside. The library is noisy and warm.

NAJIA: So, when he says "goodbye"—

AMY: He means "hello."

NAJIA: When he says your dress is "ugly"—

AMY: He means it's "pretty."

NAJIA: When he asks if I'd "hate" to be "enemies"—

AMY: He'd "like" to be "friends."

NAJIA: And he doesn't want to "leave outside"—

AMY: He wants to "go inside."

NAJIA: Because the library isn't "noisy" and "warm"—

AMY: The library is "quiet" and "cool."

NAJIA: So, what he's really saying is—

AMY: Hello, Amy, that dress is very pretty. Would you like to be friends? We can go inside. The library is quiet and cool.

NAJIA: You get it!

AMY: Sure. Very clever, Jeffrey. But you're still whacko!

(Jeffrey waves and smiles, exits left.)

NAJIA: Say, here come Pedro and Sally. Let's play Antonyms with them!

(PEDRO and SALLY enter from right, cross to center.)

AMY: Go there. I have nothing to take from you.

(Pedro and Sally are perplexed.)

PEDRO: I think Amy's been out in the sun too long!
NAJIA: We're playing Antonyms!
SALLY: Neato! Say it again!
AMY: Go there. I have nothing to take from you.
SALLY: *(pause)* Come here. I have something to give to you.
AMY: Right!
PEDRO: I've got one. My brother lost a dog when he was driving this evening.
AMY: Let me see. . . my sister found a cat when she was walking this morning.
PEDRO: You got it!

(MS. BALLANTINE, the teacher, enters from left with students BRYCE and MYRNA; they cross to center.)

SALLY: Ms. Ballantine! We're playing Antonyms!
MS. BALLANTINE: That's a great game. Would you like to play Synonyms?
AMY: How do you play that?
MS. BALLANTINE: Let's all sit down, and we'll find out.

*(Students sit in chairs as Ms. Ballantine draws a square on the chalkboard; inside the square she writes the word **near**.)*

MS. BALLANTINE: First, let's review what *synonyms* are. Who can tell us?

BRYCE: *(raises hand)* I can!

MS. BALLANTINE: Bryce.

BRYCE: Synonyms are different words that have almost the same meaning.

MS. BALLANTINE: That's correct. Who can name a synonym for "near"? As if you were using it in the sentence, "The chair was near the door." Najia, why don't you come up to the board and write the synonyms around each side of the square.

(Najia goes to the board; Myrna raises her hand.)

MS. BALLANTINE: Myrna.

MYRNA: "Close to." The chair was close to the door.

*(Najia writes **close to** at the top of the square.)*

MS. BALLANTINE: Yes. Anyone else?

(Amy raises her hand.)

MS. BALLANTINE: Amy.

AMY: "Next to." The chair was next to the door.

MS. BALLANTINE: Correct. How about you, Sally?

*(Najia writes **next to** at the bottom of the square.)*

SALLY: "Beside." The chair was beside the door.

MS. BALLANTINE: That's right. Pedro?

*(Najia writes **beside** at the left of the square.)*

PEDRO: "Bordering." The chair was bordering the door.

MS. BALLANTINE: "Bordering" is a synonym for "near."

*(Najia writes **bordering** at the right of the square.)*

MS. BALLANTINE: Very good. What's an antonym for "near"?

NAJIA: *(raises hand)* I know!

MS. BALLANTINE: Yes, Najia.

NAJIA: "Far."

MS. BALLANTINE: Correct. Write "far" underneath "near" and draw a line between them. Excellent. Now, let's play the Synonyms Game. We'll divide into two teams. Pedro, Amy and Sally are Team Number 1. Najia, Bryce, and Myrna are Team Number 2.

(Pedro, Amy and Sally move their chairs to one side of the chalkboard; Najia, Bryce and Myrna move their chairs to the other side; Ms. Ballantine stands between the two teams.)

MS. BALLANTINE: I will write a sentence on the board and underline a word. Then I will write three words, of which one is a synonym for that word. Each team has a chance to guess the correct synonym for the underlined word. If a team guesses a synonym, it earns a point. Does everyone understand how the game is played?

STUDENTS: Yes, Ms. Ballantine.

MS. BALLANTINE: Here is the first sentence. "The boat sailed on a calm sea."

*(Ms. Ballantine writes the sentence on the board and underlines **calm**.)*

MS. BALLANTINE: "Calm" is the underlined word. Here are three possible synonyms: "ordinary," "peaceful," and "deep."

*(Ms. Ballantine holds up a signboard with the words **ordinary, peaceful** and **deep**.)*

MS. BALLANTINE: Team 1?

(Team 1 members confer, whispering; Pedro raises his hand.)

MS. BALLANTINE: Yes, Pedro.

PEDRO: "Peaceful" is the synonym. The boat sailed on a peaceful sea.

MS. BALLANTINE: That's correct. In this sentence, "peaceful" is a synonym for "calm." Here's a sentence for Team 2. "The detectives found many clues in the living room."

(Ms. Ballantine writes the sentence on the board and underlines found.)

MS. BALLANTINE: "Found" is the underlined word. Here are three possible synonyms: "welcomed," "sought" and "discovered."

(Ms. Ballantine holds up a signboard with the words welcomed, sought and discovered.)

MS. BALLANTINE: Team 2?

(Team 2 members confer, whispering; Myrna raises her hand.)

MS. BALLANTINE: Yes, Myrna.

MYRNA: "Discovered" is the synonym. The detectives discovered many clues in the living room.

MS. BALLANTINE: That's correct. In this sentence, "discovered" is a synonym for "found." Both teams have a point. Here's a sentence for Team 1. "It rains very often in the spring."

(Ms. Ballantine writes the sentence on the board and underlines often.)

MS. BALLANTINE: "Often" is the underlined word. Here are three possible synonyms: "frequently," "lightly" and "quickly."

*(Ms. Ballantine holds up a signboard with the words **frequently, lightly** and **quickly**.)*

MS. BALLANTINE: Team 1?

(Team 1 members confer, whispering; Sally raises her hand.)

MS. BALLANTINE: Yes, Sally.

SALLY: "Frequently" is the synonym. It rains very frequently in the spring.

MS. BALLANTINE: That's correct. In this sentence, "frequently" is a synonym for "often." Here's a sentence for Team 2. "Butterflies begin life as caterpillars."

*(Ms. Ballantine writes the sentence on the board and underlines **begin**.)*

MS. BALLANTINE: "Begin" is the underlined word. Here are three possible synonyms: "Continue," "start" and "repeat."

*(Ms. Ballantine holds up a signboard with the words **continue, start** and **repeat**.)*

MS. BALLANTINE: Team 2?

(Team 2 members confer, whispering; Bryce raises his hand.)

MS. BALLANTINE: Yes, Bryce.

BRYCE: "Start" is the synonym. Butterflies start life as caterpillars.

MS. BALLANTINE: That's correct. In this sentence, "start" is a synonym for "begin." Both teams have two points. Let's do one final round. Here's a sentence for Team 1. "Last night I had an amazing dream."

*(Ms. Ballantine writes the sentence on the board and underlines **amazing**.)*

MS. BALLANTINE: "Amazing" is the underlined word. Here are three possible synonyms: "appealing," "astonishing" and "ascending."

*(Ms. Ballantine holds up a signboard with the words **appealing, astonishing** and **ascending**.)*

MS. BALLANTINE: Team 1?

(Team 1 members confer, whispering; Amy raises her hand.)

MS. BALLANTINE: Yes, Amy.

AMY: "Astonishing" is the synonym. Last night I had an astonishing dream.

MS. BALLANTINE: That's correct. In this sentence, "astonishing" is a synonym for "amazing." Team 1 is up by one point. Here's a last sentence for Team 2. "My cat likes to lie down in the sun."

*(Ms. Ballantine writes the sentence on the board and underlines **lie down**.)*

MS. BALLANTINE: "Lie down" is the underlined phrase. Here are three possible synonyms: "Rehearse," "relay" and "recline."

*(Ms. Ballantine holds up a signboard with the words **rehearse, relay** and **recline**.)*

MS. BALLANTINE: Team 2?

(Team 2 members confer, whispering; Najia raises her hand.)

MS. BALLANTINE: Yes, Najia.

NAJIA: "Recline" is the synonym. My cat likes to recline in the sun.

MS. BALLANTINE: That's correct. In this sentence, "recline" is a synonym for "lie down." Both teams scored the right answer for each question, so each team wins.

STUDENTS: Hurray!

(Jeffrey enters from left.)

BRYCE: Antonym Man!

(Students laugh.)

JEFFREY: I am sorry that I am late for class.

SALLY: He says, "I'm glad I'm early for class."

(Students laugh.)

JEFFREY: No, I really mean it! I *am* sorry I'm late for class. I got locked outside by accident!

MYRNA: He says he got locked inside on purpose!

(Students laugh.)

MS. BALLANTINE: Jeffrey, maybe you'd better change from Antonym Man to Synonym Man.

JEFFREY: Yes, Ms. Ballantine. I am sorry-contrite-regretful-ashamed-embarrassed-apologetic-mortified and con-science-stricken I am late for class!

STUDENTS: Hurray for Synonym Man!

(LIGHTS OUT)

THE END

mathematics

EVEN AND ODD NUMBERS
(Math)

BASIC CONCEPT:

This play defines *even* and *odd numbers* and uses them to solve addition and subtraction reasoning problems.

PRE- OR POST-PLAY ACTIVITIES:

- Draw a line on the blackboard with marks for 0, 10, 20, 30, 40, 50, 60, 70, 80, 90, 100; have students take turns filling in odd numbers, then even numbers.

- Draw a line on the blackboard from 0 to 100 with even numbers marked; randomly erase several of the even numbers, then have students fill in the missing numbers. Do this exercise for odd numbers as well.

- Draw a line on the blackboard from 0 to 96 with every eighth number marked (0, 8, 16, 24, etc.); have students fill in the number that falls midway between each marking.

- Draw a line on the blackboard from 0 to 96 with every sixth number marked (0, 6, 12, 18, etc.); have students fill in the number that falls midway between each marking.

DISCUSSION QUESTIONS:

- You are the 20th person in line at the movie ticket window, and you see your friend 10 people ahead; how many people are between you and your friend?

- Without using pencil or paper, can you determine how many even numbers are there between 15 and 51? Can you name them? How many odd numbers?

- There are 5 bags of ice in the freezer; your mother tells you to sort the bags into 3 piles, of which 2 will be an even number of bags; how many bags will you put in each of the 3 piles?

STAGE SET: a chalkboard at mid center; 4 chairs at down center

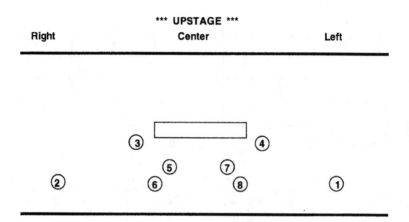

*** UPSTAGE ***

Right   Center   Left

Stage Plan — *Even and Odd Numbers*

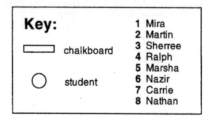

Key:		1 Mira
		2 Martin
▭	chalkboard	3 Sherree
		4 Ralph
		5 Marsha
○	student	6 Nazir
		7 Carrie
		8 Nathan

CAST: 8 actors, min. 4 boys (•), 4 girls (+)

+	Mira	•	Martin
+	Sherree	•	Ralph
+	Marsha	•	Nazir
+	Carrie	•	Nathan

PROPS: chalkboard; chalk; 7 signboards; 2 black markers

COSTUMES: characters wear contemporary school clothes; Mira and Martin wear black t-shirts and pants; Sherreè and Ralph wear white t-shirts and pants; Marsha and Nazir wear red t-shirts and black pants; Carrie and Nathan wear blue t-shirts and black pants

+	0	2	4	6	8
0					
2					
4					
6					
8					

Diagram 1

+	0	2	4	6	8
0	0	0	0	0	0
2	0	4	6	8	10
4	0	6	8	10	12
6	0	8	10	12	14
8	0	10	12	14	16

Diagram 2

+	1	3	5	7	9
1					
3					
5					
7					
9					

Diagram 3

+	1	3	5	7	9
1	2	4	6	8	10
3	4	6	8	10	12
5	6	8	10	12	14
7	8	10	12	14	16
9	10	12	14	16	18

Diagram 4

+	1	3	5	7	9
0					
2					
4					
6					
8					

Diagram 5

+	1	3	5	7	9
0	1	3	5	7	9
2	3	5	7	9	11
4	5	7	9	11	13
6	7	9	11	13	15
8	9	11	13	15	17

Diagram 6

—	9	7	5	3	1
1					
3					
5					
7					
9					

Diagram 7

—	9	7	5	3	1
1	8	6	4	2	0
3	6	4	2	0	
5	4	2	0		
7	2	0			
9	0				

Diagram 8

—	8	6	4	2	0
0					
2					
4					
6					
8					

Diagram 9

—	8	6	4	2	0
0	8	6	4	2	0
2	6	4	2	0	
4	4	2	0		
6	2	0			
8	0				

Diagram 10

—	9	7	5	3	1
0					
2					
4					
6					
8					

Diagram 11

—	9	7	5	3	1
0	9	7	5	3	1
2	7	5	3	1	
4	5	3	1		
6	3	1			
8	1				

Diagram 12

—	8	6	4	2	0
1					
3					
5					
7					
9					

Diagram 13

—	8	6	4	2	0
1	7	5	3	1		
3	5	3	1			
5	3	1				
7	1					
9						

Diagram 14

(LIGHTS UP FULL ON MIRA standing at down left and MARTIN standing at down right, facing audience; at mid center, SHERREE stands to right of chalkboard and RALPH stands to left of chalkboard, facing audience.)

MIRA: Let's talk about even and odd numbers.
MARTIN: Even numbers end in 0, 2, 4, 6 or 8.

(Sherree writes the even numbers on right side of chalkboard.)

SHERREE: The numbers 0, 2, 4 and 8 are even numbers.
MIRA: Odd numbers end in 1, 3, 5, 7 or 9.

(Ralph writes the odd numbers on left side of chalkboard.)

RALPH: The numbers 1, 3, 5, 7 and 9 are odd numbers.
MIRA: And now it's time to play—
MARTIN: "Extreme Math!"
MIRA: Featuring two teams of contestants—
MARTIN: Answering questions based on even and odd numbers.

*(Mira and Martin lead audience in applause as MAR-
SHA and NAZIR enter from right, CARRIE and
NATHAN enter from left and sit in chairs at down cen-
ter with Marsha and Nazir facing Carrie and Nathan.)*

MIRA: Team Red — Martha and Nazir!

(Audience applauds.)

MARTIN: Team Blue — Carrie and Nathan!

(Audience applauds.)

MIRA: Sherree and Ralph are the score keepers.

(Sherree and Ralph bow; audience applauds.)

MARTIN: Mira and I — Martin — are the question givers.

(Audience applauds.)

MIRA: Are you ready, Team Red?
MARTHA & NAZIR: Team Red ready!
MARTIN: Are you ready, Team Blue?
CARRIE & NATHAN: Team Blue ready!
MIRA: Let's warm up with a pre-game exercise. Team Red,
    count off even numbers to thirty starting with zero!
MARTHA: Zero!
NAZIR: Two!
MARTHA: Four!
NAZIR: Six!
MARTHA: Eight!
NAZIR: Ten!
MARTHA: Twelve!
NAZIR: Fourteen!
MARTHA: Sixteen!
NAZIR: Eighteen!

Even and Odd Numbers 45

MARTHA: Twenty!

NAZIR: Twenty-two!

MARTHA: Twenty-four!

NAZIR: Twenty-six!

MARTHA: Twenty-eight!

NAZIR: Thirty!

MIRA: That's correct!

MARTIN: Now, Team Blue, count off odd numbers to thirty starting with one!

CARRIE: One!

NATHAN: Three!

CARRIE: Five!

NATHAN: Seven!

CARRIE: Nine!

NATHAN: Eleven!

CARRIE: Thirteen!

NATHAN: Fifteen!

CARRIE: Seventeen!

NATHAN: Nineteen!

CARRIE: Twenty-one!

NATHAN: Twenty-three!

CARRIE: Twenty-five!

NATHAN: Twenty-seven!

CARRIE: Twenty-nine!

NATHAN: Thirty-one!

MARTIN: You did it, Team Blue! Now it's time for the first round of Extreme Math.

MIRA: Team Red, you're up first. Here's your question: Is the sum of two even numbers even or odd?

(Sherree holds up a signboard [Diagram 1] while Martha and Nazir confer.)

MIRA: Team Red, what is your answer?

MARTHA: The sum of two even numbers is always another even number.

MIRA: Can you prove it?

NAZIR: Yes, we can.

(Nazir fills in the numbers in the chart as shown in Diagram 2, calling out the sums as he goes.)

NAZIR: As you see from this chart, the sum of two even numbers is always even.

MIRA: That is correct. Team Red scores one point!

(Audience applauds; Nazir takes his seat.)

MARTIN: Team Blue, here is your question: Is the sum of two odd numbers even or odd?

(Ralph holds up a signboard [Diagram 3] while Carrie and Nathan confer.)

MARTIN: What is your answer, Team Blue?

NATHAN: The sum of two odd numbers is always an even number.

MARTIN: Prove it!

(Carrie fills in the numbers in the chart as shown in Diagram 4, calling out the sums as she goes.)

CARRIE: As you can see from the chart, the sum of two odd numbers is always an even number.

MARTIN: That is absolutely correct! Team Blue scores a point!

(Audience applauds; Carrie takes her seat.)

MIRA: Round two. Team Red: Is the sum of an even number and an odd number always even or always odd?

(Sherree holds up a signboard [Diagram 5] while Martha and Nazir confer.)

MIRA: Team Red, what is your answer?

MARTHA: The sum of an even number and an odd number is always an odd number.

MIRA: Can you prove it?

NAZIR: Yes, we can.

(Nazir fills in the numbers in the chart as shown in Diagram 6, calling out the sums as he goes.)

NAZIR: As you see from this chart, the sum of an even number and an odd number will always be an odd number.

MIRA: That is correct. Team Red scores a second point!

(Audience applauds; Nazir takes his seat.)

MARTIN: Moving from addition to subtraction, here is a question for Team Blue: Is the difference of two odd numbers always an even number?

(Ralph holds up a signboard [Diagram 7] while Carrie and Nathan confer.)

MARTIN: What is your answer, Team Blue?

NATHAN: The difference of two odd numbers is always an even number.

MARTIN: Prove it!

(Carrie fills in the numbers in the chart as shown in Diagram 8, calling out the differences as she goes.)

CARRIE: As you can see from the chart, the difference of two odd numbers is always an even number.

MARTIN: That is absolutely correct! Team Blue scores their second point! Extreme Math is tied!

(Audience applauds; Carrie takes her seat.)

MIRA: Next question for Team Red: Is the difference of two even numbers always even?

(Sherree holds up a signboard [Diagram 9] while Martha and Nazir confer.)

MIRA: Team Red, what is your answer?

MARTHA: The difference of two even numbers is always an even number.

MIRA: Can you prove it?

NAZIR: Yes, we can.

(Nazir fills in the numbers in the chart as shown in Diagram 10, calling out the differences as he goes.)

NAZIR: As you see from this chart, the difference of two even numbers is always an even number.

MIRA: That is correct. Team Red scores a third point to take the lead!

(Audience applauds; Nazir takes his seat.)

MARTIN: Now, to conclude the third and final round, Team Blue must correctly answer this question: Is the difference of an even number and an odd number always odd — or always even?

(Ralph holds up a signboard [Diagram 11] and Ralph holds up a signboard [Diagram 12] while Carrie and Nathan confer.)

MARTIN: What is your answer, Team Blue?

NATHAN: The difference of an even number and an odd number is always an odd number.

MARTIN: Prove it!

(Carrie goes to Sherree's signboard and fills in the numbers in the chart as shown in Diagram 13; Nathan goes to Ralph's signboard and fills in the numbers in the chart as shown in Diagram 14.)

CARRIE: This first chart shows even numbers subtracted from odd numbers. The difference of an even number and an odd number is always an odd number.

NATHAN: The second chart shows odd numbers subtracted from even numbers. But the result is the same — the difference of an even number and an odd number is always an odd number.

MARTIN: That is absolutely correct! Team Blue scores, and Extreme Math is tied!

(Audience applauds; Carrie and Nathan take their seats.)

MIRA: With both teams tied, Extreme Math goes into Special Sudden Overtime! This is where you — the audience — can play!

MARTIN: Have your teachers divide your class into teams. Then find answers to these questions based on multiplication.

SHERREE: If you multiply an even number by an even number, is the product going to be even or odd?

RAPLH: If you multiply an odd number by an odd number, is the product going to be even or odd?

SHERREE: If you multiply an even number by an odd number, is the product going to be even or odd?

RAPLH: If you multiply an odd number by an even number, is the product going to be even or odd?

MIRA: Is that a trick question?

MARTIN: Every trick is a question! So long, audience!

(All applaud; LIGHTS OUT)

THE END

LINES AND SHAPES
(Geometry)

BASIC CONCEPT:

This play defines *lines* and *shapes* and their application in basic geometry, with discussion of their use in everyday life.

PRE- OR POST-PLAY ACTIVITIES:

• Have students look through newspapers and magazines for pictures using circles and squares; cut out the pictures and sort them according to their specific shape (circle, square, rectangle, pentagon, etc.).

• Have each student draw a house on a piece of paper, using simple shapes discussed in the play; then have students identify the shapes and count them according to shape.

• Examine the houses drawn above; have students count the total number of lines and line segments in each house.

DISCUSSION QUESTIONS:

• Look around the classroom and make a list of 10 objects you see, then classify them according to their specific shape; how many objects are made up of only one shape? Two shapes? Three shapes? Are most of the objects a combination of several shapes?

• Look at the walls, ceiling, floor and windows of the classroom and the school hallways; what shapes are used in the tile, walls, glass or carpeting?

STAGE SET: any classroom

CAST: 9 actors, min. 4 boys (•), 4 girls (+)

+ Kelsey	• Carl
+ Clara	• James
+ Dorothy	• Joss
+ Brenda	• Rex
Mr. Slippers, the Cat (offstage)	

PROPS: several large sheets of white construction paper; yardstick; black marker

COSTUMES: characters wear contemporary school clothes

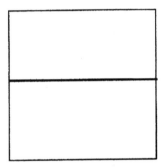

Diagram 1: line

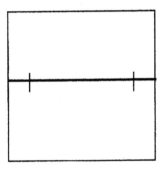

Diagram 2: line segment

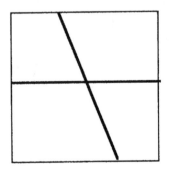

Diagram 3: angles

Diagram 4: triangle

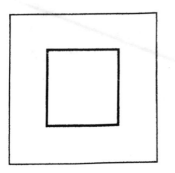

Diagram 5: square

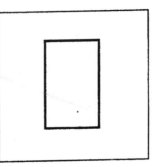

Diagram 6: rectangle

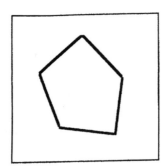

Diagram 7: pentagon

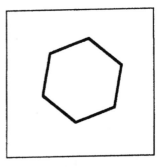

Diagram 8: hexagon

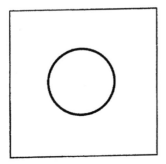

Diagram 9: circle

(LIGHTS UP FULL ON CARL kneeling at down center, facing audience; he is struggling with a yardstick and a large sheet of white construction paper; KELSEY enters from right.)

KELSEY: Carl! What are you doing?

CARL: Hi, Kelsey! I'm building a fun house for my cat, Mr. Slippers. I'm going to put all his favorite toys inside.

KELSEY: That's cool! But where are your tools? And your building materials? Where are your hammer and nails and your wood?

CARL: That all comes later. First, I have to make a plan for the house. *(scratches his head, perplexed)* This is confusing!

KELSEY: What's wrong?

CARL: I know what I *want* the house to look like. I can see it in my mind as clearly as I can see that tree over there. But I can't seem to take what's in my mind and put it on paper!

KELSEY: My mom is a carpenter. She says building something is just a matter of knowing lines and shapes.

CARL: Hey, here come some friends! Maybe they can help make a plan for Mr. Slippers' house.

(CLARA and JAMES enter from left and cross to down center.)

KELSEY: Clara and James, good to see you!

CLARA: We heard Carl's building a house for Mr. Slippers.

CARL: Yes, but I can't make a plan!

JAMES: I'd start out with the basics — lines and line segments.

KELSEY: Show us!

(James takes a sheet of paper and the yardstick and, with a black marker, draws a line across the middle with arrows at both ends — Diagram 1.)

JOSS: Here is a pentagon. *(points to sides with yardstick)* Five sides, five angles.

CLARA: And a polygon that has six sides is called—?

DOROTHY: A polygon with six sides is called a *hexagon*.

(Joss takes the marker and yardstick and draws a hexagon — Diagram 8.)

JOSS: Here is a hexagon. *(points to sides with yardstick)* Six sides, six angles.

DOROTHY: A polygon can have any number of sides. A seven-sided polygon is a *septagon*.

JOSS: An eight-sided polygon is called an *octagon*.

DOROTHY: A nine-sided polygon is called a *nonagon*.

JOSS: A ten-sided polygon is called a *decagon*.

DOROTHY: And so forth, as long as you want to keep adding sides to the closed figure.

CARL: Well, thanks, everybody. I guess I can get busy making my plan now.

BRENDA & REX (O.S.): Hold on! Wait a minute!

(BRENDA and REX enter from left and cross to down center.)

CLARA: It's Brenda!

JAMES: And Rex!

BRENDA: You've forgotten a very important shape — the circle!

REX: A circle is a closed figure, too.

BRENDA: Except the circle doesn't have sides or angles. It is just a single curved line that meets itself to form one closed figure.

(Rex takes the marker and draws a circle with a point in the center — Diagram 9.)

KELSEY: How do you measure a circle if it doesn't have sides or angles?

REX: The line of a circle is called its *circumference.* Every point on the circumference is the same distance from the center of the circle.

CARL: Now can I start making the plan for Mr. Slippers' house?

BRENDA: Not until you know all your shapes!

(Joss and Rex hold up sheets with shapes.)

DOROTHY: What's this?

(Joss holds up the triangle.)

CARL: Three sides? A triangle!

CLARA: What's this?

(Rex holds up the square.)

CARL: Four sides all the same? A square!

JAMES: What's this?

(Joss holds up the rectangle.)

CARL: Four sides with two sides the same? A rectangle!

BRENDA: What's this?

(Rex holds up the pentagon.)

CARL: Five sides? A pentagon!

KELSEY: What's this?

(Joss holds up the hexagon.)

CARL: Six sides? Has to be a hexagon!

DOROTHY: And this?

(Rex holds up the circle.)

CARL: Is a circle!

JOSS & REX: All right! Carl scores!

CARL: Finally! Now to the plan!

KELSEY: Wait a minute. Shouldn't you ask Mr. Slippers what kind of house he wants? He might have something very definite in mind.

CARL: But he's only a cat!

KELSEY: But it's his house! Maybe he likes some shapes more than others.

CARL: All right. . . where is he?

KELSEY: He was just here a minute ago playing with the yardstick.

(Everyone peers around, looking for the cat. SOUND: cat loudly meowing offstage left.)

MR. SLIPPERS (O.S.): Meow! Meow! Meow!

(Everyone looks left.)

CARL: Oh no! There he is!

KELSEY: Where? Where is Mr. Slippers?

CARL: *(points skyward)* Up there — in the tree!

(LIGHTS OUT)

THE END

science

FOSSILS
(Life Science)

BASIC CONCEPT:

This play highlights how *fossils* are created and lays the foundation for concepts of *archeology* and *prehistory* with discussion about the role of fossils in documenting how people and animals lived in the past.

PRE- OR POST-PLAY ACTIVITIES:

- Have one group of students create simple plaster casts of leaves, rocks, bones, other natural or man-made objects; call them Mystery Fossils and see if a second group of students can identify what objects made the cast imprints.

- Go outside and mark out a small patch of soft ground and carefully dig into it to see what fossils or other objects you find; then return to the classroom and make a chart that shows a cross-section of the "dig" and what was found at each level.

DISCUSSION QUESTIONS:

- What objects from our time might be found in the future?

- What would scientists in the future think about us based on these objects?

- Are some objects more likely to be preserved as fossils? Why?

STAGE SET: the edge of the playground

CAST: 9 actors, min. 4 boys (•), 5 girls (+)

+	Janelle	•	Phillip
+	Heather	•	Sean
+	Carol	•	Neal
+	Monica	•	Michael
+	Mrs. Rainer, Teacher		

PROPS: clipboard; pencil; tape measure; a pair of large rubber wading boots; large magnifying glass; trowel; plate; 2 pair of gloves; lollipop; toothpick; small table or rolling table cart; small milk carton with its top cut off; jar containing plaster of paris; jar of water; mixing stick; jar of petroleum jelly; large green tree leaf

COSTUMES: characters wear contemporary school clothes

(LIGHTS UP FULL ON PHILLIP entering from left, crossing to center stage. He wears large rubber wading boots and moves slowly in very deliberate stomps. After a particularly emphatic stomp, he faces the audience with a savage grin.)

PHILLIP: The creature walks; the earth trembles!

(JANELLE enters from right and watches Phillip for a few seconds. Then she breaks out in laughter.)

JANELLE: Phillip! What in the world do you think you're doing?

PHILLIP: I'm not Phillip — I'm a mighty brontosaurus!

JANELLE: You're a mighty dum-bo-saurus! Oooh, look at the mess you're making in the mud!

PHILLIP: I'm not making a mess, Janelle. I'm making fossils. Come on, it's fun!

(Phillip takes off his left boot and offers it to Janelle. After a moment's hesitation, she accepts it and puts it on. They stomp around center stage, as HEATHER and SEAN enter from left and watch them with amusement.)

SEAN: Look, Heather, it's that rare breed of mammal! The One-Footed Mud Stompers!

JANELLE: We're making fossils, Sean!

HEATHER: Fossils? I bet you don't even know what a fossil is! I bet you can't even spell it!

PHILLIP: Sure I can! A fossil is a footprint in the mud.

JANELLE: And it's spelled F-O-S-S-I-L. Fossil.

(Sean and Heather cross to center stage.)

SEAN: A fossil is more than a footprint in the mud. A fossil is a remain, imprint or trace of a once-living organism that is preserved in rock or in the earth's crust.

Now I Get It!

PHILLIP: Like mud. Mud is crust. And our boots have made imprints.

HEATHER: Except that a fossil has to be *preserved*. Mud will get washed away, and then your imprint is gone. It will never survive to be a genuine fossil.

(Phillip and Janelle look at each other with chagrin.)

PHILLIP: Oh. . .
JANELLE: Never mind!

(NEAL and CAROL enter from right; Neal carries a clipboard and pencil; Carol carries a tape measure; they cross to center stage and examine the footprints on the ground.)

SEAN: Hi, Neal. Hi, Carol.

HEATHER: What are you doing with that tape measure and clipboard?

CAROL: We're studying these fossils.

JANELLE: Why does anyone want to study a fossil?

NEAL: Because of what they tell you about life in the past.

PHILLIP: What can this old bootprint tell anybody?

NEAL: Fossils tell when and where certain things lived.

CAROL: And how they lived.

NEAL: Scientists can guess what ancient animals, plants and people looked like from fossils.

CAROL: Fossils can be found in rocks and ice, in tar pits and volcano craters, even in the ocean.

SEAN: Some fossils were made millions of years ago. Like dinosaur prints.

HEATHER: And dinosaur bones and teeth.

NEAL: Fossils tell us that dinosaurs lived throughout North America.

CAROL: And what plants the dinosaurs ate. When they weren't eating other dinosaurs.

NEAL: Fossils can even tell us what the weather was like in ancient times. Did you know that the continent of Antarctica once had jungles?

SEAN: Get out!

CAROL: It's true. Fossils of tropical fish and plants have been found in modern day Antarctica. And that means either the climate of the earth was much warmer—

HEATHER: Or Antarctica wasn't at the South Pole but somewhere closer to the Equator where the temperature was warmer.

(MICHAEL and MONICA enter from left; Michael carries a large magnifying glass; Monica carries a trowel and a plate; they both wear gloves.)

MONICA: Stop! Nobody move!

(Michael and Monica cross to center stage and peer intently at the ground at down center directly in front of Phillip and Janelle.)

MONICA: (points at ground next to Janelle's boot) There it is, Michael!

MICHAEL: (looks through magnifying glass at where Monica has pointed) Dig it up, Monica!

(Monica takes trowel and digs in ground; she reaches down and holds up a lollipop.)

MONICA: A fossil!

PHILLIP: Fossil? That's just an old lollipop that fell out of someone's pocket.

(Monica puts lollipop on plate; Michael pokes the lollipop with a toothpick; others gather in a semi-circle at down center as Monica passes the plate around for examination.)

Now I Get It!

MICHAEL: This organism is petrified. Definitely petrified.

MONICA: Petrified remains are very hard, like a rock.

MICHAEL: The color dye and sugar that were the basic parts of this organism have been replaced by water and quartz that made it hard as a rock.

MONICA: Then the dirt and mud formed a protective layer over the remains and kept it from dissolving or being disturbed by animals or bacteria. This organism is perfectly preserved in the same form as it was the day it was dropped.

MICHAEL: Sometimes the organism is buried under so many sediments and so much pressure and heat that it changes into carbon.

MONICA: And the carbon changes into coal.

SEAN: A lump of coal is a fossil?

MONICA: It started out millions of years ago as a bunch of dead plants.

CAROL: Look! This is a Lulubelle Lollipop. You can still see the brand name on the front.

NEAL: I haven't seen a Lulubelle Lollipop for sale in almost three years.

MICHAEL: Then this fossil is at least three years old.

HEATHER: And here are the letters M-I-L and a period at the top.

PHILLIP: That tells where the lollipop was made. They had Lulubelle Lollipop factories in Milwaukee and Memphis and Miami. M-I-L is an abbreviation for "Milwaukee."

JANELLE: The stick has diagonal lines. I remember some Lulubelle Lollipop sticks came with polka dots.

CAROL: The candy shop downtown sold the lollipops with diagonal lines on the stick.

NEAL: The drugstore at the mall sold the lollipops with polka dots.

HEATHER: This is exciting! You really can find out a lot from fossils!

(MRS. RAINER enters from left.)

MRS. RAINER: Yes, but will we ever know how it ended up in the mud?

ALL: Hello, Mrs. Rainer!

MRS. RAINER: For class today, why don't we make our own fossils? Heather and Sean, will you please bring out the experiment table?

HEATHER & SEAN: Yes, Mrs. Rainer.

(Heather and Sean bring out to down center a table; on the table is a jar of water, small milk carton with its top cut off, mixing stick, jar of petroleum jelly, jar containing plaster of paris and a large green tree leaf.)

MRS. RAINER: What materials do we have, Phillip?

PHILLIP: There is a small milk carton with its top cut off, a jar of petroleum jelly, a jar containing plaster of paris, a mixing stick and a large green tree leaf.

MRS. RAINER: Carol, why don't you pour some plaster of paris into the milk carton. Fill the carton about halfway.

(Carol fills the carton with plaster of paris.)

MRS. RAINER: Neal, if you would pour some water into the carton. . .

(Neal pours water into the carton.)

MRS. RAINER: Monica, why don't you mix the water and plaster together? Stir until it's thick and smooth. This is the sediment that will preserve our organism.

(Monica takes the mixing stick and mixes.)

MICHAEL: And the green tree leaf, Mrs. Rainer? Is that the organism we're going to make into a fossil?

MRS. RAINER: Yes, indeed, Michael. Coat the leaf with a thin layer of petroleum jelly.

(Michael coats the leaf.)

MRS. RAINER: Then press the leaf into the plaster.

(Michael presses the leaf into the plaster.)

MRS. RAINER: Good work! When we come back here this time tomorrow, we'll take the leaf out of the plaster. Then what will we have?

JANELLE: An empty space in the plaster where the leaf was.

MRS. RAINER: That empty space is called a *mold*. A mold shows the outline of the organism that was trapped in the sediment but then decayed.

HEATHER: And when sediments fill in that space?

MRS. RAINER: The sediments will be pressed against the outline of the organism and form a *cast*.

(Mrs. Rainer gazes up at the sky.)

MRS. RAINER: Uh-oh! It looks like it's going to rain. Let's go inside and continue our lesson on fossils. Sean and Heather, will you please carry in the experiment table?

HEATHER & SEAN: Yes, Mrs. Rainer.

(Heather and Sean carry the table off left as Mrs. Rainer and the other students follow her off left — except for Phillip who can't get his boot out of the mud.)

PHILLIP: Hey, wait up! *(struggles to move but can't)* Hey, guys! Unnnh! Can I get a hand here? Mrs. Rainer! *(struggles)* Unnnh! Anybody have a tractor? *(stops moving, looks at audience in despair)* I'm only in third grade! I'm too young to become a fossil!

(LIGHTS OUT)

THE END

VITAMINS
(Human Body)

BASIC CONCEPT:

This play defines *vitamins* and introduces basic nutritional principles related to normal mealtime diet.

PRE- OR POST-PLAY ACTIVITIES:

- Have students make a chart listing several common foods they eat; consult a dietary handbook and find the calorie content for the foods. Make a similar chart listing fat content.

- Do a food-fat test using a potato chip, carrot, chocolate candy bar, piece of cooked hamburger, banana, cookie, orange juice, whole milk, skim milk, and butter. Take a brown paper bag and cut it into small squares, labeling each square with the name of the food. Rub or drip some of each food on its square and let the squares dry. Hold each square up to the light; the spotted squares contain fat. Which squares are spotted? Which are not?

DISCUSSION QUESTIONS:

- Bring in several Nutrition Facts labels from commercial food products and make a chart of the vitamins contained in them; which vitamins are most common? Are there certain foods that contain no vitamins? Why?

- Make a chart listing the chief vitamins; which vitamins are fat-soluble and which are water-soluble?

STAGE SET: a table, 2 chairs and a trash container at down left; bench at down right

CAST: 15 actors, min. 2 girls (+)

+	Sharon	+	Deanna
	Vitamin A		Vitamin B1
	Vitamin B2		Vitamin B3
	Vitamin B6		Vitamin B12
	Vitamin C		Vitamin D
	Vitamin E		Vitamin K
	Folate		Biotin
	Pantothenic Acid		

PROPS: candy bars; bubblegum and candy pieces; soft drink can; brown paper lunch sack; plastic bowl of soup; several celery and carrot sticks; oat-bran muffin; banana; cheese sandwich with tomato slice and lettuce; small milk carton; spoon; napkins; science book; orange; lime; lemon; potato; paperback book

COSTUMES: Sharon and Deanna wear contemporary school clothes; Vitamins wear t-shirts and jeans with their vitamin sign or vitamin name displayed on their shirt front.

(LIGHTS UP FULL ON SHARON sitting at table at down left; she is eating a large candy bar and sipping from a soda can. DEANNA enters from right, carrying a brown paper lunch sack, and crosses to the table.)

DEANNA: Hi, Sharon!
SHARON: Hi, Deanna! Sit down and eat lunch with me.
DEANNA: Thanks!

(Deanna sits and opens her lunch sack, pulling out a plastic bowl containing soup, several celery and carrot sticks, an oat-bran muffin, a banana, a cheese sandwich with tomato and lettuce and a small carton of milk.)

SHARON: Wow, that's a lot of food. Didn't you eat breakfast?
DEANNA: I always eat breakfast. And when it's lunch time, I eat a few small things to keep up my energy for the afternoon. I've got chicken noodle soup, a banana, some celery and carrot sticks, a cheese sandwich with tomato and lettuce. And for dessert, a really tasty oat-bran muffin I'll wash down with some milk. What did you have for lunch?
SHARON: *(holds up candy bar)* You're looking at it! *(pops final bite into her mouth)*
DEANNA: You're kidding! All you had for lunch was a candy bar?
SHARON: *(shrugs)* I don't like to make a big deal out of eating. Can I borrow a napkin? Thanks. *(takes a napkin, wipes her fingers and mouth)*
DEANNA: Sharon, if all you're eating for lunch is a candy bar, you're going to get really sick!
SHARON: No way! This candy bar contains plenty of sugar and starch. They make carbohydrates, and they make calories, and that makes energy, right? I need *lots* of energy, especially with this science test tomorrow.

DEANNA: Sure, carbohydrates do turn into calories, and that does give you a burst of energy — for a little while, anyway. But you need much more besides carbohydrates to be healthy.

SHARON: What else?

DEANNA: Vitamins, for one thing. Vitamins are an important source of nutrients for human beings.

SHARON: Will they give me lots of energy?

DEANNA: They don't give a big instant charge of energy like sugar and starch. But vitamins help the body do lots of things, like process the other nutrients you take in while you eat. Sure you don't want a celery stick?

SHARON: *(grimaces)* Celery? Gag-a-rama! *(takes a big gulp of her soda and deposits the can in the trash container)* I'd better use this energy while it's hot. I'm going to study in the park. See you!

DEANNA: Bye!

(Deanna packs up her lunch and exits left as Sharon crosses to down right and sits on the bench; Sharon opens her book on her knee but begins to get sleepy and nod off.)

SHARON: *(jerking awake)* Whoa! I'm getting really sleepy! All those calories are supposed to keep me awake!

(VITAMIN A enters from right and stands behind Sharon, peering over her shoulder at her book.)

SHARON: *(rubbing her eyes)* The print in this book is too small! *(looks toward sky)* Darn clouds! How can I read when it's this dark?

VITAMIN A: *(pops in front of her)* Guess you're going to need me!

SHARON: *(jumps, startled, brandishes book)* Waaah! Stand back or I'll—

VITAMIN A: But you need me!

SHARON: I need you to jump off a bridge! Get away!

VITAMIN A: No, Sharon, you need me to read that book!

SHARON: I can read!

VITAMIN A: But your eyes are sore and you don't see well in poor light. I can help.

SHARON: Are you an eye doctor?

VITAMIN A: No, I'm Vitamin A. *(proudly points to A on chest)*

SHARON: You're Vitamin A? *(laughs)* Right, and I'm the Red Queen in Alice in Wonderland!

VITAMIN A: Vitamin A maintains healthy skin, bones, teeth and hair. And helps you see better in dim light. You're having trouble reading because you don't have enough Vitamin A — that's me — in your diet.

SHARON: Do you live around here?

VITAMIN A: Sure! You can find me in eggs and cheese, vegetables and fruit and, of course, milk.

(Sharon starts coughing and develops a hacking spasm.)

(VITAMIN C enters from right and crosses to Sharon, patting her on the back.)

VITAMIN C: There, there, Sharon.

SHARON: *(coughing subsides)* Who are you?

VITAMIN C: I'm Ascorbic Acid!

SHARON: What?

VITAMIN C: But you can call me Vitamin C! Sounds like you're getting a cold. I can help.

SHARON: *(sneezes)* Aaaahhh-choo!

VITAMIN C: *(takes an orange from pocket and offers it to her)* Here!

SHARON: *(sniffs)* An orange? I think I need a handkerchief.

VITAMIN C: One of the best sources of Vitamin C is found in citrus fruits like oranges, limes, lemons.

(Sharon takes orange.)

VITAMIN A: And don't forget tomatoes.

VITAMIN C: That's right! And potatoes!

(Vitamin C takes lime, lemon and potato from pocket and piles them onto Sharon's hands; she juggles and drops them.)

SHARON: Hey!

(VITAMIN D, VITAMIN E and VITAMIN K enter from right and cross to Sharon, glancing at her critically.)

VITAMIN D: Hmmm. Not very strong, can't even hold a potato!

SHARON: Says who?

VITAMIN D: *(bows)* Vitamin D, to the rescue! I've got the calcium you need to build up those puny bones. You'll find me every time you drink a glass of milk, eat a slice of liver or even take a walk in the sunlight.

VITAMIN E: *(takes Sharon's finger and examines it)* Just checking to see if you cut yourself on that nasty lemon.

SHARON: *(pulls finger away)* And you are?

VITAMIN E: *(bows)* Vitamin E, at your service. If you don't have enough of me, your red blood cells will rupture. You'll find me in margarine and vegetable oils, whole grains and wheat germ.

VITAMIN K: *(waves hello to Sharon)* I'm Vitamin K. I help your blood clot better when you get a cut or bruise. You'll find me in green, leafy vegetables — spinach, cabbage and kale.

VITAMIN E: Me, too! And, lucky for you, I — along with mis amigos Vitamins A, D, K — are *fat-soluble.*

SHARON: Fat-what?

VITAMIN C: Fat-soluble means the vitamins dissolve in fatty tissue, which means they can be stored in your body. Vitamin C, on the other hand, is a *water-soluble* vitamin, which your body cannot store—

VITAMIN C: *(grabs Sharon's hand)* You can't live a single day without me, sister!

(VITAMIN B1, VITAMIN B2, VITAMIN B3, VITAMIN B6 and VITAMIN B12 enter from left, arm-in-arm and cross to center.)

VITAMIN A: Look, here come the B Vitamins!

VITAMIN B1: I'm Vitamin B1. I'm essential for absorbing carbohydrates in your body. And I prevent damage to your nervous system.

VITAMIN B2: I'm Vitamin B2. I help oxidize carbohydrates.

VITAMIN B3: I'm Vitamin B3. I help prevent pellagra and aid in energy metabolism.

VITAMIN B6: I'm Vitamin B6. You better eat lots of meat, poultry and fish, so I can help your skin stay healthy.

VITAMIN B12: Vitamin B12, here. I'm essential for keeping your blood healthy. Like my fellow Vitamin Bs, you can find me in meat and eggs and cheese.

(FOLATE, PANTOTHENIC ACID and BIOTIN dash in from left.)

FOLATE: Hold on, we're B Vitamins, too!

(Folate, Pantothenic Acid and Biotin shake Sharon's hand.)

FOLATE: I'm Folate. I fight anemia.

PANTOTHENIC ACID: Pantothenic Acid, glad to meet you. You need me for passing nerve signals throughout your body.

BIOTIN: And I'm Biotin. I help your heart stay strong.

(All the Vitamins converge around Sharon, trying to pull her to go with them.)

VITAMIN A: Here, Sharon, you need your Vitamin A.

VITAMIN C: Don't forget Vitamin C!

VITAMIN D: Come on, we'll take a walk in the sunshine, get some Vitamin D.

VITAMIN B1 & VITAMIN B2: Hey, she needs her B Vitamins!

VITAMIN B3: She needs a *lot* of B Vitamins; B Vitamins are water-soluble!

(Sharon shakes herself free at down center.)

SHARON: Wait a minute! How am I supposed to get through the day with all of you vitamins following me around?

VITAMIN E: Simple; just eat the right kind of foods.

VITAMIN K: Foods that have us vitamins living inside.

VITAMIN B3: We'll help you get all the nutrients you need from every bite or sip.

SHARON: That sounds great! It's a deal! *(shakes hands with Folate, Pantothenic Acid and Biotin)*

VITAMIN B6: Not so fast, young lady. *(holds out hand)* Fork it over.

SHARON: What-what-what are you talking about?

VITAMIN B12: Don't play the lamb with us, Sharon. Surrender your junk food — or else!

(Sharon takes out a string of candy bars, bubble gum, candy treats from her pockets and reluctantly gives them to Vitamin B6 and Vitamin B12, who hold them up for display and handle them with disgust, as the other Vitamins shrink back in horror and begin to exit right.)

VITAMIN B6: Not one single one of us lives in this stuff!

VITAMIN B12: If this was the biggest part of your daily diet, you'd be sick *all* the time!

(Deanna enters from left and sits at table, sipping from her milk carton and reading a paperback book; all the Vitamins exit right except for Vitamin A.)

SHARON: But I'm hungry!

VITAMIN A: *(points to Deanna)* There's your friend. She probably has something good to eat. Ummm, carrot stick, yum-yum! Lots of Vitamin A! *(exits right)*

(Sharon crosses to table.)

SHARON: Hi, Deanna!

DEANNA: Hi, Sharon! How did your studying for the science test go?

SHARON: Studying? Gee, I guess didn't get any studying done at all. But I sure learned a lot! Say, do you have anything to eat?

DEANNA: I'm sorry, Sharon. I don't have any candy bars or—

SHARON: No, I mean, a carrot stick. Or maybe a slice of tomato. Real food!

DEANNA: *(pauses to regard Sharon with wonder and puzzlement)* Wow, you're right, Sharon. . . you really *did* learn a lot!

(LIGHTS OUT)

THE END

THE PLANETS
(Earth Science)

BASIC CONCEPT:

This play introduces the *planets* of our solar system, defining them in terms of *surface temperature*, *atmosphere*, *orbital path*, *size* and *distance from the Sun*.

PRE- OR POST-PLAY ACTIVITIES:

- Have students create a chart listing important dates and discoveries in astronomy and space exploration.

- Make a chart that compares the characteristics of the planets: surface temperature, atmosphere, orbital path, size and distance from the Sun.

- Make color drawings of the planets (or mount color photographs) and discuss what factors give each of the planets its own distinct color.

DISCUSSION QUESTIONS:

- As of this writing in November, 1999, five more planets on the edge of our solar system just beyond Pluto have been discovered. What names would you give them?

- The technology used in modern space exploration has produced many materials and inventions that are used in our daily lives — sunglasses that adjust to different light levels, fire-resistant uniforms for firefighters, a device that helps visually-impaired people read currency. Can you name others?

- Some scientists believe the Earth's moon was formed when a large space object collided with Earth and threw off particles of gas and dust to create a new mass. Others believe the moon was a small space object that wandered into the orbit of the Earth. A third theory says that the moon was formed by loose material floating in space after the birth of our solar system. Which theory do you think might be true and why?

STAGE SET: a bench at down right; floor space with approximately 12' x 12' of open area; positions of Sun and Planets marked on floor; orbit paths of Planets around Sun marked on floor

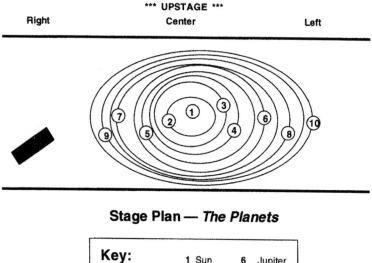

Right   *** UPSTAGE *** Center   Left

Stage Plan — *The Planets*

Key:		
▮ bench	1 Sun	6 Jupiter
	2 Mercury	7 Saturn
	3 Venus	8 Uranus
① planet	4 Earth	9 Neptune
	5 Mars	10 Pluto

CAST: 14 actors, min. 1 boy (•), 1 girl (+)

+   Mia
     Sun
     Venus
     Mars
     Saturn
     Neptune
     Copernicus, the Robot

•   Max
     Mercury
     Earth
     Jupiter
     Uranus
     Pluto
     Professor Meadows

COSTUMES: Max and Mia wear contemporary school clothes; the Sun and Planets each wear a t-shirt that has the body's name on the front; Copernicus is attired in a robot outfit; Professor Matthews wears a white lab coat over standard shirt and slacks

(LIGHTS UP DOWN RIGHT ON MAX and MIA sitting on a bench at down right; they are gazing up at the sky.)

MAX: Look at those stars, Mia! There are so many, as far as the eye can see!

MIA: Some of those stars are actually planets, Max. *(points left)* Tonight our teacher said you can see two planets, Venus and Mercury, in that part of the sky.

MAX: Where?

MIA: Over there to the southeast, just above the horizon. Mercury is below the Moon, and Venus is that really bright star above the Moon to the right.

MAX: I see them! Wow! Don't you wish you could travel to the planets?

MIA: That would be incredible.

COPERNICUS (O.S. LEFT): Well, what are we waiting for? Let's go!

(Max and Mia look at each other, perplexed.)

MAX: Did you hear that?

MIA: That weird, creepy voice in the darkness? No, I didn't hear anything! Nothing at all!

(LIGHTS UP FULL as COPERNICUS, a robot, enters from left and crosses to center.)

COPERNICUS: Greetings, students! My name is Copernicus. I am a robot. I work with Professor Meadows at the observatory down the road.

(Startled at first, Max and Mia become curious and venture closer to the robot.)

MAX: What are you doing here?

COPERNICUS: Just looking at the stars, same as you.

MIA: Your name is Copernicus? That was the name of the 16th-century Polish astronomer who discovered that the planets in our solar system revolve around the Sun.

COPERNICUS: That is correct. You know a lot about astrononmy — for a human. If you want to learn more, come with me!

(SUN, MERCURY, VENUS, EARTH, MARS, JUPITER, SATURN, URANUS, NEPTUNE and PLUTO enter from left; they are huddled together in a mass and move slowly toward center.)

COPERNICUS: The universe is in constant change. Our solar system was formed about five billion years ago, give or take a million or twenty. An enormous cloud of gas, ice and dust was spinning around in space, spinning very slowly.

(Sun and Planets stop at mid center and spin slowly in a clockwise direction.)

COPERNICUS: A nearby star may have exploded, sending shock waves into the cloud that caused it to begin spinning faster.

(Sun and Planets spin slightly faster, still clockwise.)

COPERNICUS: The enormous cloud began to shrink in on itself, or *contract*, and the temperature at the center of the cloud became very hot — about ten million degrees! That is when the process of nuclear fusion started and parts of the cloud were thrown off from the center.

(Planets spin off and circle around Sun.)

COPERNICUS: The hot center of the cloud became the Sun. The gas and dust and ice particles out in space began to merge and come together into solid matter. Over time, they formed into planets.

(Planets stop in their positions, facing audience.)

MAX: Where does the word planet come from?

COPERNICUS: The word "planet" comes from a Greek word meaning "to wander," and that is just what planets do — except that they wander along a fixed route called an *orbit*.

MIA: Do they always go in circles around the sun?

COPERNICUS: That's what everyone thought until the 1600s, when the German astronomer Kepler discovered that the planets orbit the sun in an oval-shaped pattern that's called an *ellipse*. They also orbit at different speeds. Which planets do you think travel the fastest?

MAX: The ones closest to the sun?

COPERNICUS: That is correct. Let us look at the Sun and the planets in our solar system.

SUN: I am the Sun, a star made up of gas. I contain over ninety-nine per cent of all the matter in the solar system. I produce energy by fusing hydrogen into helium in my center, or *core*. Temperatures in my core are around twenty-seven million degrees. Tempertures on my surface are as high as ten thousand degrees. The light and heat I give off extend millions of miles through space. It takes about eight minutes for my light to reach the Earth.

MERCURY: Mercury is the closest planet to the Sun, about thirty-six million miles away. I am also the eighth-largest planet. My atmosphere is composed of hydrogen, helium, sodium and potassium. My surface temperature averages three hundred thirty-three degrees. It takes eighty-eight Earth days for me to orbit the Sun.

VENUS: Venus is the second planet from the Sun, about sixty-seven million miles away. I am the sixth-largest planet. My entire surface is covered by dense clouds, and my atmosphere is mostly carbon dioxide. My surface temperature averages nine hundred degrees. It takes two hundred twenty-five Earth days for me to orbit the Sun.

EARTH: The Earth is the third planet from the sun, about ninety-two million miles away. I am the fifth-largest planet in the solar system. My atmosphere is composed mostly of nitrogen, oxygen and argon. My surface temperatures average forty-five degrees, and I have one moon. It takes approximately three hundred sixty-five days for me to orbit the Sun.

MARS: I am Mars, fourth planet from the Sun, about one hundred twenty-eight million miles away. I am the seventh-largest planet in the solar system. My atmosphere is composed mostly of carbon dioxide, with some nitrogen and argon. My surface temperature averages minus seventy-six degrees, and I have two moons. It takes six hundred eighty-eight Earth days for me to orbit the Sun.

COPERNICUS: Mercury, Venus, Earth and Mars are the inner planets of the solar system. Now, we come to the outer planets.

JUPITER: Jupiter is the fifth planet from the Sun, about four hundred sixty million miles away. I am the largest planet. My atmosphere is composed mostly of hydrogen, helium, ammonia and methane. My surface temperature averages minus one hundred sixty degrees, and I have sixteen moons. It takes almost twelve Earth years for me to orbit the Sun.

SATURN: Saturn is the sixth planet from the Sun, about eight hundred thirty-seven million miles away. I am the second-largest planet. My atmosphere is composed mostly of hydrogen, helium, ammonia and methane. The rings that surround me are made of rock and ice. My surface temperature averages minus two hundred twenty degrees, and I have eighteen moons. It takes twenty-nine and a half Earth years for me to orbit the Sun.

URANUS: Uranus is the seventh planet from the Sun, about one point seven million miles away. I am the third-largest planet. My atmosphere is composed mostly of hydrogen, helium and methane. Like Saturn, I also have rings, but they are very thin and dark and cannot be seen from the Earth. My surface temperature averages minus three hundred twenty degrees, and I have fifteen moons. It takes eighty-four Earth years for me to orbit the Sun.

NEPTUNE: I am Neptune, eighth planet from the Sun, almost two point eight million miles away. I am the fourth-largest planet. My atmosphere is composed mostly of hydrogen, helium and methane. My surface temperature averages minus three hundred thirty degrees, and I have eight moons and a few rings. It takes nearly one hundred sixty-five Earth years for me to orbit the Sun.

PLUTO: I am Pluto, the ninth planet in the solar system, almost two point eight million miles away. I am the smallest planet and sometimes my orbit takes me closer to the Sun than my neighbor Neptune. Like Neptune, my atmosphere is composed mostly of hydrogen, helium and methane. My surface temperature averages minus three hundred seventy degrees, and I have one moon called Charon that some people think is actually a tenth planet. It takes nearly two hundred forty-eight Earth years for me to orbit the Sun.

COPERNICUS: There you have it — the planets of our solar system!

MIA: That's really neat. Say, Copernicus, can you tell us about asteroids and comets and supernovas?

COPERNICUS: Oh, sure! Heck, I'm just getting warmed up!

(PROFESSOR MEADOWS enters from left and spies Copernicus.)

PROFESSOR MEADOWS: There you are!

COPERNICUS: Uh-oh! Busted!

(Copernicus starts to amble offstage right as Professor Meadows crosses to center in pursuit.)

PROFESSOR MEADOWS: Don't let that robot get away!

(*Copernicus halts.*)

COPERNICUS: Gee, Professor, can't a fellow take an evening stroll?

PROFESSOR MEADOWS: First, you're not a fellow, you're one of the world's most intelligent, advanced robots. Second, you're needed back at the observatory — we think we may have discovered a new planet.

MAX & MIA: A new planet? Can we come see?

PROFESSOR MEADOWS: Maybe later. Right now, I've got to get Copernicus home.

COPERNICUS: Robots don't get vacation time!

MAX: So long, Copernicus! Thanks for telling us about the planets!

MIA: And don't forget, Professor — we want to come to the observatory and look at the new planet!

(*Professor Meadows leads Copernicus offstage left; LIGHTS FADE DOWN AND OUT WITH SPOTLIGHT ON Max and Mia sitting on bench at down right.*)

MAX: Gosh, imagine that! We met a real robot!

MIA: And a real astronomer!

MAX: Do you think there are any more planets left to discover in our solar system?

MIA: (*leans back and gazes up at sky*) If there are, I'm going to try and find them.

MAX: Yeh, me, too. It sure beats watching television.

(*LIGHTS OUT*)

THE END

social studies

HOME SWEET BIOME
(Geography)

BASIC CONCEPT:

This play highlights the *biome* and lays the foundation for concepts of *ecosystem* and discussion about the impact of human beings on natural environments.

PRE- OR POST-PLAY ACTIVITIES:

- Have students create mini-biomes in the classroom that can serve as parts of the stage set — simple representations of plants, animals, house structures, geographic features.

- Making costumes native to each biome should also be incorporated.

- Students can make charts that give the characteristics of each biome.

DISCUSSION QUESTIONS:

- What type of biome do we live in?

- What climate characteristics does our local biome have?

- What sort of unique animals live in our biome?

- What kind of plants and trees grow in our biome?

- Why did people come to settle in our locality?

- Was our local biome the same before people came to live in it as it is now?

- How has our biome changed over time?

- Will it change more in the future?

In addition, you may want more than two Explorer Teams and more than two sets of actors to handle the biome roles, depending upon class size. You may also want to have the rest of the class ("Audience") participate during the play rather than waiting until the end as is scripted here.

STAGE SET: any classroom; each biome is a defined area, possibly 4' x 4' square at most; each biome can have platforms or scrims or props hanging from above

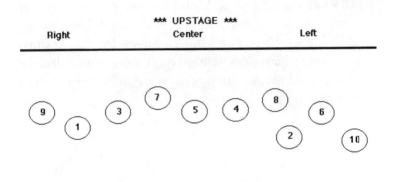

Stage Plan— *Home Sweet Biome*

Key:			
	1 Tropical Rain Forest	6	Cool Grassland
	2 Tropical Grassland	7	Desert
(1) biome	3 Mediterranean	8	Tundra
area	4 Temperate Forest	9	Arctic
	5 Cool Forest	10	High Mountain

CAST: 12–36 actors, min. 2 boys, 2 girls

> 2 Narrators
> 10 sets of 3 actors in each biome (minimum of 2 sets of 3 actors)
> 2 Explorer Teams
>> Team 1: Lucy and Lamont
>> Team 2: Moira and Duane

PROPS: 2 pair of binoculars; 2 clipboards; 2 pens; 2 pair of sunglasses; pair of gloves; scarf

MUSIC: *Home Sweet Home*

COSTUMES: Lucy, Lamont, Moira and Duane wear explorer attire — any combination of wading/hiking boots, field/down jackets, pith helmets, camouflage/khaki shirts and pants; Narrators wear formal suits and/or dresses; biome actors wear clothing appropriate to their climate and region

Home Sweet Biome

(from "Home Sweet Home", words by John H. Payne,
music by Henry R. Bishop, arranged by L.E. McCullough)

(SPOTLIGHT ON NARRATOR #1 standing at down right, facing audience.)

NARRATOR #1: Welcome, members of the Global Geography Society. Today, two teams of explorers will venture into uncharted areas of our planet. They will be given clues about their location and then must decide in what *biome* they find themselves.

(SPOTLIGHT ON NARRATOR #2 standing at down left, facing audience.)

NARRATOR #2: What is a biome? A biome is a natural ecology region that has a special set of landforms, bodies of water, climate and forms of plant and animal life unique to that region.

NARRATOR #1: Our planet has ten main biome systems.

NARRATOR #2: And the explorer teams will visit each one, trying to identify the biome type.

(SPOTLIGHT ON LUCY and LAMONT entering from right and crossing to down center; Lucy carries a pair of binoculars, Lamont carries a clipboard and pen.)

NARRATOR #1: Explorer Team Number One, Lucy and Lamont!

(Audience applauds; SPOTLIGHT FOLLOWS Lucy and Lamont as they cross to Biome 1 and begin scrutinizing it.)

BIOME 1/ACTOR #1: This biome is located near the equator. The climate is hot and rainy all year round with sometimes as much as two hundred inches of rain a year.

BIOME 1/ACTOR #2: The hot, rainy climate allows a large number of different plant and animal species to grow, including hundreds of types of trees, most of them hard-woods like ebony and rosewood.

LUCY: Look at how tall the trees grow!

LAMONT: And they grow so close together!

BIOME 1/ACTOR #3: In this biome trees grow so close that their tops form a *canopy* — a thick blanket of leaves and branches. This canopy prevents sunlight from penetrating to the ground.

LUCY: Look at the plants near the bottom of the trees. Their leaves are wide and flat.

LAMONT: That's probably so they can take in as much sun as possible.

BIOME 1/ACTOR #1: Many of the animals in this biome live in trees. They include many types of birds — toucans, parrots, macaws and eagles.

BIOME 1/ACTOR #2: Reptiles like snakes and crocodiles.

BIOME 1/ACTOR #3: And mammals like bats, monkeys, flying squirrels and leopards.

LUCY: I've got it! This biome is a Tropical Rain Forest!

NARRATOR #1: That is correct! Explorer Team Number One has identified the first biome — a Tropical Rain Forest!

(Audience applauds.)

NARRATOR #1: And where on our planet can you find a Tropical Rain Forest biome?

LAMONT: Tropical Rain Forest biomes are found in Africa and Central and South America.

LUCY: And in many parts of southeast Asia such as Thailand, Vietnam, Malaysia and Indonesia.

(SPOTLIGHT ON DUANE and MOIRA entering from left and crossing to down center; Duane carries a pair of binoculars, Moira carries a clipboard and pen.)

NARRATOR #2: Explorer Team Number Two, Duane and Moira!

(Audience applauds; SPOTLIGHT FOLLOWS Duane and Moira as they cross to Biome 2 and begin scrutinizing it.)

BIOME 2/ACTOR #1: This biome is also located near the equator, but they have a wet season and a dry season. Rainfall averages no more than forty inches a year, and the temperature is hot most of the year.

BIOME 2/ACTOR #2: Very few trees live here, and the plants are mostly thick grasses that can live without much rainfall.

BIOME 2/ACTOR #3: The grasses cover large plains and provide food for animals such as antelopes and zebras.

BIOME 2/ACTOR #1: Buffalo and giraffes.

BIOME 2/ACTOR #2: Gazelles and rhinoceroses.

BIOME 2/ACTOR #3: Vast herds of wildebeests.

DUANE: *(peers through binoculars)* Look, there's an elephant!

MOIRA: Is that a cheetah? Look at how fast it runs!

DUANE: The cheetah is the fastest animal on land. Say, there's a pride of lions chasing away a pack of hyenas!

MOIRA: This biome is a Tropical Grassland!

NARRATOR #2: That is correct! Explorer Team Number Two has identified the second biome — a Tropical Grassland!

(Audience applauds.)

NARRATOR #2: And where on our planet can you find a Tropical Grassland biome?

DUANE: Tropical Grassland biomes are found in Africa and South America.

MOIRA: And in northern Australia.

(SPOTLIGHT ON Lucy and Lamont examining Biome 3.)

NARRATOR #1: Explorer Team Number One arrives at the third biome!

BIOME 3/ACTOR #1: This biome is located along the sea-coast. Rainfall averages no more than ten inches a year, and the temperature is hot in the summer and cool in the winter.

BIOME 3/ACTOR #2: Very few trees live here, and they are mostly evergreens.

BIOME 3/ACTOR #3: Along with many small bushes and hardy grasses.

LAMONT: Look, there is a fox stalking a field mouse!

LUCY: *(points upward)* And a hawk seizing a rabbit!

LAMONT: I think this is a Mediterranean Biome!

NARRATOR #1: That is correct! Explorer Team Number One has identified the third biome — a Mediterranean Region!

(Audience applauds.)

NARRATOR #1: And where on our planet can you find a Mediterranean biome?

LAMONT: All around the Mediterranean Sea, of course — the coastal areas of Spain, France, Italy, Greece, Turkey, Israel, Lebanon and all of North Africa.

LUCY: And parts of Northern California and western Chile that border the Pacific Ocean.

(SPOTLIGHT ON Duane and Moira examining Biome 4.)

NARRATOR #2: Explorer Team Number Two arrives at the fourth biome!

DUANE: *(points upward)* Gosh, look at these incredibly tall trees!

MOIRA: I see oak and elm. . .

DUANE: Ash, maple and birch. . .

MOIRA: And this — this is a giant sequoia, one of the tallest trees in the world!

BIOME 4/ACTOR #1: This biome is filled with forests and is generally located midway between the equator and the polar regions.

BIOME 4/ACTOR #2: This biome has warm summers and cool winters, with an average rainfall of about forty inches a year.

BIOME 4/ACTOR #3: Many types of animals live here in the shade of the large trees — songbirds, deer, owls, raccoons and possums.

DUANE: From the evidence I see, this biome is a Temperate Forest!

NARRATOR #2: That is correct! Explorer Team Number Two has identified the fourth biome — a Temperate Forest!

(Audience applauds.)

NARRATOR #2: And where on our planet can can you find a Temperate Forest biome?

MOIRA: Temperate Forest biomes are found in the northern United States and in parts of Europe, Russia and China.

(SPOTLIGHT ON Lucy and Lamont examining Biome 5.)

NARRATOR #1: Explorer Team Number One arrives at the fifth biome!

BIOME 5/ACTOR #1: This biome also has many forests, with pine, spruce and hemlock trees.

BIOME 5/ACTOR #2: But this biome is much colder and has much less rainfall — only about twenty inches a year. Summer is short, and winter is long in this biome.

BIOME 5/ACTOR #3: The animals in this biome include moose, elk, wolf and bear. They often hibernate during the coldest part of the winter.

LUCY: From the evidence I see, this biome is a Cool Forest!

NARRATOR #1: That is correct! Explorer Team Number One has identified the fifth biome — a Cool Forest!

(Audience applauds.)

NARRATOR #1: And where on our planet can you find a Cool Forest biome?
LAMONT: In Canada and Russia.

(SPOTLIGHT ON Duane and Moira examining Biome 6.)

NARRATOR #2: Explorer Team Number Two arrives at the sixth biome!
DUANE: *(peers through binoculars)* I see nothing but grass for miles!
MOIRA: The grass is almost as tall as small trees!
BIOME 6/ACTOR #1: This biome has few trees and is covered with an abundance of grass and wild flowers.
BIOME 6/ACTOR #2: Shootingstars, yarrows, sunflowers.
BIOME 6/ACTOR #3: Most of this biome is no longer wild but is used for farming and raising livestock.
MOIRA: This is a Cool Grassland biome!
NARRATOR #2: That is correct! Explorer Team Number Two has identified the sixth biome — a Cool Grassland!

(Audience applauds.)

NARRATOR #2: And where on our planet can you find a Cool Grassland biome?
DUANE: Every continent has some area that is a Cool Grassland biome.
MOIRA: The prairie region of the United States.
DUANE: The pampas region of Argentina.
MOIRA: Parts of southeast Africa and eastern Europe.
DUANE: The steppes of southern Russia and northern China and eastern Australia.

(MUSIC: Home Sweet Home.)

ALL: *(sing)* Amid tundras and grasslands
  Wherever we roam,
  Be it ever so humble,
  There's no place like home.

  Landforms and changing climates
  Shape nature's grand design,
  With many types of species
  From bugs to humankind.

  Home, home, sweet sweet biome,
  Be it ever so humble,
  There's no biome like home.

(LIGHTS OUT)

THE END

A CHILD'S DAY
IN RURAL AMERICA, 1876
(History)

BASIC CONCEPT:

This play explores the life of a typical farm family in late 19th-century America, highlighting the need for self-sufficiency and inter-dependence with discussion of the significant role children played in the household economy.

PRE- OR POST-PLAY ACTIVITIES:

- Re-create your classroom as a rural classroom in the year 1876. What would the building look like? What would be the sources of heat and light and water? Would you have a desk? What writing and reading materials would you have available? Would everyone have books of their own?

- Draw the types of houses (inside and outside) farmers lived in during the 1870s on the Midwestern prairie — wood, sod, stone. Make a list of household objects that would have been in the kitchen, parlor, bedroom.

- Make a chart of foods that would have been available to a farm family in the 1870s. Where would they have gotten their food? How would they have prepared it?

DISCUSSION QUESTIONS:

- What are some of the daily chores children performed in the 1870s?

- Did boys and girls have separate types of chores? Why?

- Think of some chores children do today that children did in 1876; would you be able to do them the same way then as you do now? What would be different?

- When Edith reached thirteen, she did not go back to school. Why?

- Where did farm families in 1876 get news of current events?

STAGE SET: at right is a wooden cot; at center is a fireplace with a rocking chair, a small food preparation table, a larger eating table, a chair and 2 stools; at left is a bench and a teacher's writing desk

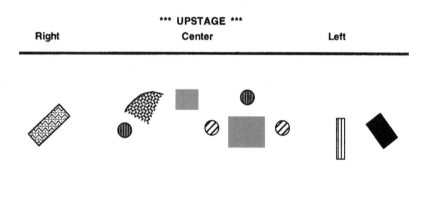

*** UPSTAGE ***

| Right | Center | Left |

Stage Plan — *A Child's Day in Rural America, 1876*

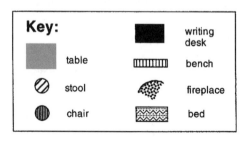

Key:

table		writing desk	
stool		bench	
chair		fireplace	
		bed	

CAST: 8 actors, min. 3 boys (•), 5 girls (+)

+ Edith
+ Esther
+ Eliza
+ Miss Greeley

• Wesley
• Ervin
• Mr. Webster, Father
+ Mrs. Webster, Mother

PROPS: 2 buckets; fireplace poker; bread dough; pie pan; cooking pot; coffee pot; ladle; 3 plates; 3 cups; 3 spoons; 3 knives; 2 aprons; washing pan; wash stick; 2-3 pieces of firewood; water dipper; sewing needle; darning needle; 5 licorice sticks; bouquet of flowers

MUSIC: *Skip to My Lou*

COSTUMES: characters wear 1870s rural farm clothing — wool collarless shirt, wool trousers, boots and flat-brimmed straw or felt hat for Mr. Webster and boys; plain long farm dresses, wool stockings, simple brogan shoes, bonnets for Mrs. Webster and girls; Miss Greeley wears slightly more "store-bought" dress and shoes

Skip to My Lou
(traditional, arranged by L.E. McCullough)

Lou, lou, skip to my lou; Lou, lou, skip to my lou;

Lou, lou, skip to my lou; Skip to my lou, my dar- ling

Lit- tle red wa-gon, paint it blue; Lit- tle red wa- gon, paint it blue;

Lit- tle red wa-gon, paint it blue; Skip to my lou, my dar- ling

(STAGE IS DARK. SOUND: dripping water from a leaky roof.)

ELIZA: Not again! When is this rain going to stop!

(LIGHTS UP RIGHT ON ELIZA at mid right sitting on the edge of her bed, a simple cot or woodframe bed. MRS. WEBSTER enters from right.)

MRS. WEBSTER: What is the matter, Eliza?

ELIZA: Mother, the roof is leaking again! And it woke me up from the most wonderful dream!

MRS. WEBSTER: It is almost an hour before sunrise — time you were up to start your chores.

ELIZA: Can father fix the leak?

MRS. WEBSTER: Father is already out in the barn harnessing the oxen for plowing. The roof will have to wait till tonight.

ELIZA: I can hardly wait till our new house is ready. Imagine — living in a house that's made out of wood and not lumps of packed-together dirt!

MRS. WEBSTER: That is enough complaining, Eliza. We are very lucky to have this nice sod house. It keeps us warm in winter and cool in the summer.

ELIZA: And wet every time it rains!

MRS. WEBSTER: Go get a bucket from the yard and put it under the leak. Wesley can stuff some straw in the ceiling. Help me move your bed out of the way so I can get breakfast ready.

(Eliza and Mrs. Webster move the bed upstage; EDITH enters from right, tying on an apron, and addresses audience.)

EDITH: Dear Diary. My name is Edith Webster, and that is the way our day is starting at the Webster farm outside St. Ansgar, Iowa — the twelfth of May, 1876, the one hundredth year of the United States of America. I am fourteen years old, the eldest child. My sister Eliza — who you heard whimpering about a little water on her forehead — is twelve. Then there are the boys, Wesley and Ervin —

(WESLEY and ERVIN enter groggily from right, rubbing the sleep from their eyes.)

WESLEY: Wesley Webster, howdy. *(yawns)*
ERVIN: Ervin Webster, hullo. *(yawns)*
EDITH: Who are eleven and ten years old — as well as being the laziest humans in the State of Iowa.
ERVIN: Hey now!
WESLEY: What did Preacher Gillespie say last Sunday about calling folks names?
EDITH: And then there is Esther, the youngest; she is nine years old.

(ESTHER enters from right, bringing a bucket to Eliza; Wesley stands on a stool and mimes stuffing straw into the ceiling above the bed.)

ERVIN: Esther is not our blood sister. We adopted her when her parents both died of consumption two winters ago.
WESLEY: But she is very clever and just about the best candle dipper in all Mitchell County! Far better than old "fumble fingers Edith"!

(Edith sticks out her tongue at Wesley.)

EDITH: I will keep that in mind when I mend your trousers.
ERVIN: Mother says so, too!
EDITH: You see the degree of patience an eldest child must possess! Everyone to your chores and hurry! You are going to school today!
WESLEY: Oh, boy! I love school!

ERVIN: I hope my friend Tommy Whittaker gets to come to school today. He has the biggest cat's-eye marble in the entire thirty-eight United States of America!

WESLEY: I am going to draw water from the well for mother to cook and wash with. Then I will clean out the milking stalls.

ERVIN: I am going to sharpen the knife father uses for butchering hogs. Then I will chop a cord of wood for the fire.

(Wesley and Ervin exit right.)

ELIZA: I am going to milk the cows and prepare the washing tub and stitch up a hole in father's vest.

ESTHER: I am going to feed the chickens and gather eggs for selling in town at the end of this month. And then I'll hunt for some wild berries to use in a pie mother is making for the quilting bee next Saturday.

(Eliza and Esther exit right; LIGHTS UP CENTER as Edith crosses to small table next to fireplace.)

EDITH: And I am going to bake the cornbread for dinner. And help mother weed the vegetable garden. And skin the rabbits Wesley shot by the creek — their fur will make a nice pair of work gloves for father.

(Mrs. Webster crosses to center and takes on an apron from the back of a chair; she ties it on and crosses to fireplace, takes a poker and stirs up the embers; Edith kneads bread dough.)

MRS. WEBSTER: Eliza is right. It is going to be much more pleasant when we move into the new house. It will even have a separate kitchen, with an iron stove all the way from Chicago!

EDITH: And windows — with real glass! But we do live a lot nicer than many of our neighbors. Some of them barely have a roof over their heads, hardly more than a hole dug out in the side of a hill. There just are not very many trees on the prairie to use for timber! But when father and mother got our land in the Homestead Act and moved here from Pennsylvania, they built a two-room sod house with a thatch roof that has lasted five whole years! Father helped build fortifications in the War between the States, you know, and he learned how to make many useful things.

(Mrs. Webster takes a cooking pot from the fire and stirs it with a ladle.)

MRS. WEBSTER: Breakfast is ready, Edith. Better set the table.

(MR. WEBSTER enters from right with Ervin and Wesley following; they sit at table — Mr. Webster in chair at head of table — as Edith puts 3 sets of plates, cups, spoons and knives on the table.)

MR. WEBSTER: Good morning, all. Mmm, the salt pork and coffee smell delicious!

ERVIN: And johnnycakes! Yum!

WESLEY: Is there any molasses left? Johnnycakes taste the bestest with molasses!

(Mrs. Webster dishes out food on plates; Edith serves coffee; as the men eat, Edith returns to kneading bread dough and Mrs. Webster)

MRS. WEBSTER: That is "best" not "bestest," Wesley. What sort of grammar do they teach at your school?

ERVIN: He is always too busy thinking about food. He would eat his *McGuffey's Reader* if he could!

MR. WEBSTER: Now there, we have plenty of food to go around. Your mother and sisters see to that. Eat hearty, boys. After you come home from school we have a lot of raking to do in the cornfield.

ERVIN: And Wesley and I are going to put up our new scarecrow.

WESLEY: It looks just like that clown we saw when the circus came to town last year. Do you think the circus will come back this year, father?

MR. WEBSTER: I expect so. But we will have to see that all the crops are harvested before we make any promises about the circus.

ERVIN & WESLEY: Yes, sir.

(Mr. Webster, Ervin and Wesley finish eating, rise from table and exit right; Eliza and Esther enter from right and sit at the table, joined by Edith; Mrs. Webster serves their food on the same plates, and the girls begin eating.)

ELIZA: I found a nice patch of mallows growing in a shade patch by the creek — purple and pink.

ESTHER: They will look pretty in the bonnet I am making for Lita Olson's cornhusk doll.

EDITH: You youngsters ought to be reviewing your spelling lessons. How do you spell "electricity"?

ELIZA: That is not a word, Edith! You made it up!

EDITH: It is so a word! Tell her, mother!

MRS. WEBSTER: Edith is right. Electricity is a force of nature. Just like fire and water and wind.

ELIZA: Then Edith must be a force of nature. She has more wind than a cyclone in June.

(Edith sticks out her tongue at Eliza.)

MRS. WEBSTER: At the barn raising in Toeterville last month, Mrs. Tuttle the merchant's wife told me she recently read in a newspaper from back East that electricity may someday be used to light our lamps. Imagine that!

EDITH: I hope it smells better than kerosene and buffalo chips!

(Eliza, Esther and Mrs. Webster laugh.)

MRS. WEBSTER: Eliza and Esther, it is time you got ready for school. It is almost six o'clock!

(Edith collects the plates and puts them in a washing pan on the fireplace hearth; Eliza and Esther rise from table and exit right.)

EDITH: I wish I could still go to school. But when I turned thirteen, I had to stay home and help mother with the housework. Like washing clothes.

MRS. WEBSTER: I will go outside and build the fire. Then I will hang the wash kettle over the fire and pour water from the well into the kettle.

EDITH: When the water is hot, mother will pour in a helping of lye soap I made last week. And then I take the wash stick and stand at the kettle for two or three hours, pushing and poking the clothes with the wash stick while mother starts getting the food ready for father's mid-day dinner.

MRS. WEBSTER: After I have set some beans to boil and baked up the batch of cornbread Edith prepared this morning, I will help pound and dry the clothes.

EDITH: We take the clothes out of the kettle and lay them out on a battling bench. Then we take big wooden paddles and pound the dirt out of the clothes.

MRS. WEBSTER: Then we rinse the clothes three times to get the soap out and then wring the water out by hand.

EDITH: If it does not rain till evening and the wind keeps up, we might be able to get all the clothes dry today.

MRS. WEBSTER: I think the weather today is going to be very fine, Edith. Let us begin!

EDITH: I wonder if someday they will ever make a machine that uses electricity to wash and dry clothes?

MRS. WEBSTER: You have such an imagination! Why, I am sure they will invent a machine that flies in the air first!

(Mrs. Webster and Edith exit right; LIGHTS DOWN RIGHT AND CENTER; LIGHTS UP LEFT ON SCHOOLROOM; MISS GREELEY sits behind writing desk; Eliza and Ervin sit on bench, each holding a school book in hand.)

ELIZA: Miss Greeley, where are the other children?

MISS GREELEY: The Donnelly twins are ill with the measles. Emily and Tommy Whittaker have to help their father with planting. And with all the rain, the Vanderstel family probably cannot get their wagon across the muddy roads.

ERVIN: Gosh, they should forget the old wagon and try walking. They live a couple miles closer than us, and we walk six miles to school and back every day!

MISS GREELEY: We are all very impressed by your dedication to scholarship, Master Webster. When I was a girl in Ireland, we had no school buildings at all. We met by the roadside in small gaps among the hedgerows that divided the fields. There was not one book among us, but we learned Greek, Latin and French. *And* Etiquette.

(Esther enters from left carrying a bucket of water with a dipper, which she places up left; Wesley enters behind her carrying 2–3 pieces of firewood, which he places down left.)

MISS GREELEY: Thank you for gathering the water and firewood, children. Now, please take up your reading books. Esther, would you recite the first poem?

(Esther stands, peering at the book with difficulty and struggling to focus.)

MISS GREELEY: Is there a problem, Esther?

ESTHER: Miss Greeley, it is very dark, and I cannot see the words very clear.

MISS GREELEY: *Clearly* — use the adverb, please. Yes, it is indeed a very dark day, and our window is very small. You may move closer to the fire, Esther.

ESTHER: Thank you, Miss Greeley.

(Esther moves closer to the fire and begins to read.)

ESTHER: The Brook Song. By James Whitcomb Riley. "Little brook! Little brook! You have such a happy look. Such a very merry manner, as you swerve and curve and crook. And your ripples, one and one, reach each other's hands and run like laughing little children in the sun."

MISS GREELEY: That is very good, Esther. You may sit down. With only three months to a school term, there are many areas of learning we will not have time to fully explore. Reading, writing, history, geography are the most important for general knowledge, and to these we have given much attention. However, in the years to come, an understanding of science will be necessary for both men and women, be they city-dwellers or plowers of the fields. And so, we commence our study of arithmetic. Please take out your slates, and let us begin memorizing the tables of multiplication.

(LIGHTS OUT LEFT; LIGHTS UP CENTER ON Mrs. Webster sitting in the rocking chair and Edith sitting at the table; they are sewing and mending clothes.)

MRS. WEBSTER: This has been a hard year on clothes. Both boys have grown so much, I have had to make almost twice the number of shirts I made the two years previous. It seems like I am always making or mending clothes.

EDITH: And making a shirt is no easy task. Father has to trade a pig for enough wool, then mother cards and spins the wool and weaves and sews the entire shirt, from collar to tail — even making the buttons by hand!

MRS. WEBSTER: The last two shirts I made for the boys were a nice warm brown color. I made the dye from walnut hulls Edith found by the creek.

EDITH: A traveling shoemaker came to St. Ansgar last spring and made father a nice pair of boots. And mother says there is a dry goods store in Mason City that sells cloth already made and colored! Just imagine!

MRS. WEBSTER: Edith, your dress is getting a bit frayed at the hem. We might cut it back for Eliza to wear.

EDITH: Goody! Then I can have a new dress of my own?

MRS. WEBSTER: Probably one of my old ones until I have time to make something new.

EDITH: We never waste any clothing in this family. When mother's dress wears, she cuts it back to fit me. Then it gets cut again for my younger sisters. When they wear it through, it gets cut into dish rags. And when they get too thin, we weave the strips into rag rug like that one there. *(points to floor)*

(LIGHTS UP RIGHT as Ervin, Eliza, Wesley and Esther rush in from right and gather around the main table.)

ERVIN: It is really beginning to rain! Cats and dogs!

WESLEY: And elephants, too! Those last few drops felt like hailstones!

ELIZA: Was father able to fix the leak over my bed?

EDITH: Yes, he did, right after dinner.

MRS. WEBSTER: I expect we will have an early supper so father can get in a longer day of work tomorrow. Tend to your chores now, while I get the fire ready for cooking.

(Mrs. Webster crosses to center and ties on her apron; at the fireplace, she takes a poker and stirs up the embers; Edith sets the table with plates, cups and utensils; Ervin and Wesley cross to down right; Eliza and Esther cross to down center.)

ERVIN: After we finish our afternoon chores, we are free to have fun!

WESLEY: Ervin caught a prairie dog once.

ERVIN: Tried to make it a pet, but it ran away.

WESLEY: Fishing is always fun. Ervin and I catch plenty of fish — even without a pole!

ERVIN: You just slap up the water with your hands till the fish get scared and jump into a frog hole on the bank.

WESLEY: All you have to do then is reach in and pull out your fish!

ERVIN: And hope no water moccasin is in that hole, too!

ELIZA: Esther and I make dolls.

ESTHER: Sometimes father lets us use his hunting knife, and we carve wooden toys.

ELIZA: At school we play jump rope and hide-and-seek.

ESTHER: On nice days we have picnics and go berry-picking.

WESLEY: And pitch horseshoes. *(flings an imaginary shoe toward audience)*

ERVIN: At night after supper, we often play checkers.

ELIZA: And jacks.

ESTHER: And ring-around-the-rosy and pop-the-whip and statue. *(points at Eliza)* Freeze!

(Eliza freezes in a silly position.)

WESLEY: I am known as one of the best marble shooters in the county!

ERVIN: Pshaw! And one of the biggest tall-tale tellers!

ESTHER: Storytelling is one of our favorite things. Father and mother have some wonderful stories about growing up in the forest in Pennsylvania.

ELIZA: And riddles. *(to Esther)* Four fingers and a thumb, yet flesh and bone I have none?

ESTHER: A glove! *(to Ervin)* What is red and blue and purple and green? No one can reach it, not even a queen?

ERVIN: A rainbow in the sky, the last I have seen! *(to Wesley)* What flies forever, rests never and is never caught?

WESLEY: The wind, the wind, or so I thought. *(to Eliza)* What was born when the world was made, but older than a month never grows?

ELIZA: The moon up above; why, look how it glows! *(to Esther)* And how much, how much is the moon above worth?

ESTHER: A dollar; it has four quarters, of that I am sure. *(to Ervin)* Tell me, brother dear, what has a heart in its head?

ERVIN: You must mean lettuce — green, purple or red. *(to Wesley)* Then, what has a head but not any hair?

WESLEY: A pin or a nail; have you some to spare? *(to Eliza)* What has a head but cannot think?

ELIZA: Could be a match laying on the kitchen sink?

EDITH: As the eldest child, I no longer partake in silly games. *I* write poems in my diary. *(whispers loudly to audience)* One of these days, I will send them to the town newspaper and be a published poet like Elizabeth Barrett Browning!

(Mr. Webster enters from right with both hands hidden behind his back.)

MR. WEBSTER: I hear there is a quilting bee to be held in this house.

MRS. WEBSTER: All the neighbors for miles around will attend. The women will stitch together several quilts to welcome the new family from Denmark that moved in down the road.

MR. WEBSTER: That sounds like a mighty important event. I expect we had better get ourselves in shape.

WESLEY: Fiddlesticks! Here come more chores!

MR. WEBSTER: Maybe so, but first we are going to need some extra nourishment. *(shows his right hand, filled with licorice sticks)*

ERVIN: Licorice sticks!

(Ervin, Wesley, Eliza and Esther crowd around Mr. Webster as he hands out licorice sticks; Edith pretends she is not interested.)

WESLEY: Each one cost a whole penny!

ELIZA: Thank you, father!

ESTHER: This is a wonderful treat!

MR. WEBSTER: There is one left with your name on it, Edith.

EDITH: No thank you, father, I no longer have a taste—

(Mr. Webster waves the stick in front of Edith's nose, and she begins to weaken.)

ERVIN: Come on, sis — let down your hair!

EDITH: Very well! *(grabs the stick)* I will show you how a poet eats candy! With elegance and grace! *(nibbles briefly, then stuffs the stick in her mouth)*

ALL: *(laughing)* Way to go, sis! That's showing 'em! Yahoo!

(Mr. Webster crosses to Mrs. Webster, and shows his left hand, which holds a bouquet of colorful wildflowers.)

MR. WEBSTER: *(bows)* And something for Mrs. Webster.

MRS. WEBSTER: *(takes the flowers, curtsies)* Why, thank you, Mr. Webster.

(Ervin, Wesley, Eliza, Esther and Edith begin clapping and singing as Mr. Webster and Mrs. Webster dance arm-in-arm at down center. MUSIC: "Skip to My Lou.")

ERVIN & WESLEY (SING)
> Lou, lou, skip to my lou
> Lou, lou, skip to my lou
> Lou, lou, skip to my lou
> Skip to my lou, my darling

ELIZA, ESTHER & EDITH (SING)
> Little red wagon, paint it blue
> Little red wagon, paint it blue
> Little red wagon, paint it blue
> Skip to my lou, my darling

ERVIN & WESLEY (SING)
> Fly's in the buttermilk, shoo, fly, shoo
> Fly's in the buttermilk, shoo, fly, shoo
> Fly's in the buttermilk, shoo, fly, shoo
> Skip to my lou, my darling

ELIZA, ESTHER & EDITH (SING)
> Cows in the wheatfield, two by two
> Cows in the wheatfield, two by two
> Cows in the wheatfield, two by two
> Skip to my lou, my darling

ALL (SING)
> Lou, lou, skip to my lou
> Lou, lou, skip to my lou
> Lou, lou, skip to my lou
> Skip to my lou, my darling

(LIGHTS OUT)

THE END

WHAT A GOVERNMENT DOES
(Citizenship)

BASIC CONCEPT:

This play highlights *government functions and services* and introduces basic principles of civic responsibility with discussion of the *common good, individual and group rights* and *role of laws.*

PRE- OR POST-PLAY ACTIVITIES:

- Have students make a chart listing 3 rules at their home and 3 rules at school; discuss why these rules exist.

- Each student is suddenly elected Supreme Ruler of his/her own country; have each make a list of the 5 most important rules he/she will enact right away and explain why they are the most important.

- Make a chart of the chief elected and appointed officials in your community; describe their job duties and to whom they are responsible.

DISCUSSION QUESTIONS:

- Take a walk with students through the neighborhood; what things or services do they see that are paid for by tax money? Why?

- Find a newspaper or magazine article on local people in your community who have been designated as "good citizens"; why were they chosen? What characteristics should a "good citizen" have?

- Sometimes a business or company is referred to as "a good corporate citizen." What does this mean? In what ways does a company act like an individual? What are the responsibilities a company has to the community?

STAGE SET: table at mid left with 3 chairs

CAST: 25 actors, min. 1 boy (•), 1 girl (+)

+ Joy
 4 Soccer Players
 Policeman
 Highway Surveyor
 Street Sweeper
 Animal Control Worker
 Swimming Pool Attendant
 Job Training Tutor
 Hospital Nurse
 Auto License Clerk

• Wendell
 3 Family Members
 Fireman
 Public Records Clerk
 Health Clinic Doctor
 Public Housing Supervisor
 School Band Director
 Preservation Specialist
 Water Dept. Engineer
 Restaurant Inspector

PROPS: soccer ball; 3 dinner plates; plastic food items; surveying tool; push broom; animal control stick net; test tube vial; conductor baton; lifeguard whistle; marriage license

COSTUMES: Joy, Wendell and Family Members wear contemporary school clothes; Soccer Players wear soccer outfits; Policeman, Fireman, other government workers wear attire appropriate to their occupation along with suitable props (whistle for Swimming Pool Attendant, baton for School Band Director, marriage license for Public Records Clerk, etc.)

(LIGHTS UP FULL ON WENDELL standing at down right; he is practicing a speech, using emphatic hand and facial gestures.)

WENDELL: And as your Supreme Ruler, I will not hesitate to be redundant or repetitive.

(JOY enters from right and watches him for a moment, puzzled.)

JOY: Are you trying out for the school play, Wendell?

WENDELL: What? Oh, hi, Joy. No, I'm practicing my first speech as Supreme Ruler. When I grow up, I'm going to have my own country! *(strikes a regal pose)* Wendell the First!

JOY: That's cool. What kind of government are you going to have?

WENDELL: Government? What do you mean?

JOY: I mean, every country has a government.

WENDELL: Why?

JOY: Because every country — or any group of people living together — needs rules, or laws. And you need a government to make those laws.

WENDELL: In *my* country, we won't need laws. Everyone will just do what I say!

JOY: Sorry, Wendell. It doesn't work that way. Open up your eyes and smell the popcorn!

(FOUR SOCCER PLAYERS enter from left and cross to down center; PLAYER #1 carries a soccer ball.)

PLAYER #1: All right, our team kicks off. Then your team has five plays to reach goal.

PLAYER #2: Wait a minute, we get six plays to reach goal.

PLAYER #3: I think *we* should kick off.

PLAYER #1: What are you talking about? You're on *my* team.

PLAYER #3: No, I'm not. We never chose teams.

PLAYER #2: That goal is too small. We want a bigger goal.

PLAYER #4: Every time you score, you get three points.

PLAYER #3: Uh-uh. Two points, except when you score during the last minute of the quarter.

PLAYER #1: We don't have quarters. We only play halves.

PLAYER #2: Give me the ball! *(grabs ball from Player #1)*

PLAYER #1: No, *we* kick off! *(grabs ball back)*

PLAYER #3: Just throw it up in the air and get started!

PLAYER #4: Don't throw it, kick it!

PLAYER #2: This is a stupid game. I'm going home. *(exits left)*

PLAYER #3: Me, too. *(exits left)*

PLAYER #1: You can't quit!

PLAYER #4: Why not? There isn't any rule that says I can't! *(exits left)*

(Player #1 stamps foot and marches off left.)

JOY: Did you see what happened? The game didn't have any rules, so no one could play. Everybody lost.

WENDELL: Games are silly. In *my* country, they won't be allowed. So, why will I need a government?

JOY: Rules and laws aren't just for games. They're needed for every activity people do together, from operating a business to driving on the highway to living in a family.

(THREE FAMILY MEMBERS enter from left and sit at table; each carries a plate with various plastic food items.)

MEMBER #1: Gee, this calabash looks really tasty!

(Member #2 takes a piece of food from Member #1's plate.)

MEMBER #1: Hey, what are you doing?

MEMBER #2: I just took your calabash. I'm going to eat it. *(chews)* Mmm, you're right, it is tasty!

MEMBER #3: I don't think he wants you to take his calabash.

MEMBER #2: Who's going to stop me? Is there a rule that says I can't take food when I want it?

MEMBER #3: *(shrugs)* No.

MEMBER #2: Okay.

(Member #2 takes a piece of food from Member #3's plate; Member #3 takes a piece of food from Member #1's plate.)

MEMBER #1: Hey!

(Member #2 and Member #3 take all the food from Member #1's plate.)

MEMBER #1: If everyone takes my food, I'll starve!

MEMBER #3: *(shrugs)* So? More food for me.

(Three Family Members exit left, carrying plates and squabbling.)

WENDELL: My older brother is like that. Always trying to grab every cookie on the table.

JOY: But your family has rules for mealtime, right?

WENDELL: Sure. Mom makes him finish his vegetables before he can have *any*thing for desert.

JOY: And if you didn't have that rule—

WENDELL: He'd chew our legs off!

JOY: So having rules at mealtime prevents your brother from taking your cookie?

WENDELL: Definitely!

JOY: And helps your brother learn better table manners?

WENDELL: We can hope.

JOY: And makes sure that everyone in your family gets their fair share of food?

WENDELL: You bet!

JOY: So, the rules aren't good just for you, or for your brother. . . they're good for everybody?

WENDELL: Right.

JOY: That's the purpose of laws. They protect the rights of the individual and of the group. They protect the "common good." And the government—

WENDELL: Makes sure the laws are obeyed.

JOY: Just like your parents make sure your family obeys the mealtime rules. A government has police and courts and jails to do that, instead of moms and dads and time-outs. The government protects your rights as a citizen.

WENDELL: I see. What else does a government do?

JOY: A government provides services to its citizens.

WENDELL: Services? You mean like washing windows?

JOY: Sometimes, if the windows belong to a public building. Look, here come some government services now!

(POLICEMAN, FIREMAN, HIGHWAY SURVEYOR, STREET SWEEPER, ANIMAL CONTROL WORKER, PUBLIC RECORDS CLERK, HEALTH CLINIC DOCTOR, PUBLIC HOUSING SUPERVISOR enter from left and stand in line at down left facing audience; SWIMMING POOL ATTENDANT, SCHOOL BAND DIRECTOR, JOB TRAINING TUTOR, PRESERVATION SPECIALIST, WATER DEPARTMENT ENGINEER, HOSPITAL NURSE, AUTO LICENSE CLERK, RESTAURANT INSPECTOR enter from right and stand in line at down right facing audience; each government worker steps forward to say his/her lines.)

JOY: A Policeman.

POLICEMAN: Pardon me, ma'am, but which way on South Street did the burglar make his escape?

WENDELL: A Fireman.

FIREMAN: There's a big column of smoke pouring out of the old spinach factory! All units to the scene!

JOY: A Highway Surveyor.

HIGHWAY SURVEYOR: *(measuring with surveying tool)* We'll have this new traffic signal put up by the end of summer.

WENDELL: A Street Sweeper.

STREET SWEEPER: *(holding a large push broom)* We keep the streets so clean you could eat off the pavement!

JOY: An Animal Control Worker.

ANIMAL CONTROL WORKER: *(brandishing a stick net)* Don't worry, sir, we'll catch that loose dog that bit your son.

WENDELL: A Public Records Clerk.

PUBLIC RECORDS CLERK: Welcome to Public Records. Would you like a marriage license today? How about a birth certificate? Zoning permit? Fishing license?

JOY: Health Clinic Doctor.

HEALTH CLINIC DOCTOR: We've had forty-two cases of measles the last week. It's time to issue a public health alert and vaccinate every child at risk.

WENDELL: A Public Housing Supervisor.

PUBLIC HOUSING SUPERVISOR: I'm very sorry to hear about the flood that destroyed your home. You may stay in a public housing apartment until your new house is ready.

JOY: A Swimming Pool Attendant.

SWIMMING POOL ATTENDANT: Our city has a great park system, and a new indoor swimming pool open all year round.

WENDELL: A School Band Director.

SCHOOL BAND DIRECTOR: *(waving baton)* Pay attention, trumpets! We're competing in the All-State Concert Finals next week!

JOY: A Job Training Tutor.

JOB TRAINING TUTOR: I'm sorry you were laid off from your job. Here at the new technology training center, we'll teach you skills for another job you'll like even more.

WENDELL: A Preservation Specialist.

PRESERVATION SPECIALIST: George Washington ate breakfast in this old house. It would make a great museum and would bring people to our city from all over the world.

JOY: A Water Department Engineer.

WATER DEPARTMENT ENGINEER: *(holds up a test tube vial)* It's my job to make sure the water we drink is clean and safe.

WENDELL: A Hospital Nurse.

HOSPITAL NURSE: Our emergency room is open twenty-four hours a day, every day in the year. Hope we don't see *you* anytime soon!

JOY: An Auto License Clerk.

AUTO LICENSE CLERK: No, sir, you do not need a license to drive your horse in your field, but you *do* need a license to drive your horse trailer on a public street.

WENDELL: A Restaurant Inspector.

RESTAURANT INSPECTOR: I make sure your food not only tastes good but is good for you.

JOY: Those are just a few of the many services a government provides to its citizens.

WENDELL: That's great. But who pays all those people to provide those services?

JOY: The government pays them.

WENDELL: And who pays for the government?

JOY: We all do.

WENDELL: Me? Why should I pay for the government?

JOY: If you use the services a government provides, you should help pay for them.

WENDELL: What about my rights as a citizen?

JOY: Every citizen has responsibilities as well as rights. And one of those responsibilities is to pay taxes that contribute money to the common good. Remember the "common good," Wendell?

WENDELL: I guess my having clean water and good schools and safe streets *is* part of the common good.

JOY: And don't forget an indoor swimming pool at the city park.

WENDELL: That's all right. As long as *I'm* running the government.

(Wendell steps to down center and strikes a regal pose.)

WENDELL: And as your Supreme Ruler, I will not hesitate to have taxes on Monday, Wednesday and Friday.

JOY: *(to audience)* You know, I think we're going to need another lesson in government *really* soon.

(LIGHTS OUT)

THE END

"GET ME INFORMATION, PLEASE!"
(Current Events)

BASIC CONCEPT:

This play highlights *sources of information about current events* with discussion about how news is gathered, processed and distributed via major print and broadcast media.

PRE- OR POST-PLAY ACTIVITIES:

• Have each student make a list of 3 current events; ask from what news source(s) students learned about the event.

• Visit a library and take a tour of the reference material resources: encyclopedias, CD-ROMS, photo archives, video and audio tape collections, etc.

• Select a local current event (an election, a sporting event, a business opening or closing, weather emergency, etc.) and have students make a list of what reference sources they would use to obtain information about the event.

DISCUSSION QUESTIONS:

• Watch a short video clip of a news event broadcast on television, then read a newspaper article on the same event; what are the differences in how the event was described? Did some facts receive more or less emphasis in the different media?

• Have students make a chart listing the job duties of a newspaper reporter and a television reporter; how are they the same, and how are they different?

• Find articles on the same event from a newspaper, a magazine and the Internet; what are the differences and similarities in the articles? If there are major differences, what do you think are the reasons?

STAGE SET: any classroom; wheeled cart at mid center

CAST: 15 actors, min. 1 boy (•), 1 girl (+)

+	Erika	•	Gary
	Television		Radio
	Newspaper		Internet
	Magazine		Videotape
	CD-ROM		Audiotape
	Book		Reporter
	Editor		Designer
	Printer		

PROPS: newspaper; small radio; television channel changer; computer mouse; audio cassette; videotape; CD-ROM; magazine; book; notepad; pencil; micro-cassette recorder; photo camera; video camera; cell telephone; laptop computer; sheet to cover items on cart

COSTUMES: characters wear contemporary school clothes

(LIGHTS UP FULL ON ERIKA and GARY standing at down center, addressing audience; behind them at mid center is a wheeled cart covered with a sheet.)

ERIKA: The times we live in are often referred to as "The Information Age." What is information, and how do we get it?

GARY: Information is knowledge. Knowledge is based on facts. If you know facts about something, you have information about it. You can have information about people, places, things — and events.

ERIKA: How do you get information about an event? An event like the big rainstorm that came through town last night?

GARY: You can get information about an event from many sources. These sources are called *media*. They are businesses that gather information and then distribute it for people to buy.

(NEWSPAPER and RADIO enter from left and stand at down left; TELEVISION and INTERNET enter from right and stand at down right; Newspaper holds a newspaper, Radio holds a small radio, Television holds a television channel changer, Internet holds a computer mouse.)

NEWSPAPER: You can read about the big storm in a daily newspaper.

RADIO: You can hear about the storm on a radio broadcast.

TELEVISION: Television will show you moving pictures and sounds of the big storm. It can even show you the storm as it is actually happening.

INTERNET: The internet can broadcast sounds and pictures about the storm on your computer, and you can read about it there, too.

GARY: Newspapers, radio, television and the internet — those are the media that give us information as the event happens or very close to when it happened.

ERIKA: What if I want more information about the event later? Information that gives more detail about the storm — how it came to be and what its effects were afterwards?

GARY: You want information sources you can study over and over.

(MAGAZINE and AUDIOTAPE enter from left and stand at down left in front of Newspaper and Radio; VIDEOTAPE and CD-ROM enter from right and stand at down right in front of Television and Internet; Magazine holds a magazine, Audiotape holds an audio cassette, Videotape holds a videotape, CD-ROM holds a CD-ROM.)

MAGAZINE: A magazine is a printed collection of written articles like those in a newspaper, except a magazine article about an event can be larger and contain more words and pictures.

AUDIOTAPE: An audiotape gives you all the sounds of an event. You listen to an audiotape in an audio cassette player.

VIDEOTAPE: A videotape gives you sounds and moving pictures. You watch and listen to a videotape in a video cassette player.

CD-ROM: A CD-ROM has sound, video and written articles about the event. You watch, hear and read a CD-ROM in a computer.

(BOOK enters from left, dashing onstage hastily and rushing to down center.)

BOOK: Don't forget me! I'm a book — one of the best ways to learn all about what happened in great detail! They started printing me in China around eleven hundred years ago and over five hundred years ago in Europe. I do just as good a job of giving facts now as I ever did!

GARY: You can buy all of these items from the companies that produce them, but you can also find them at your local library or even a museum.

ERIKA: Who gathers information for the media?

(REPORTER and EDITOR enter from left and stand at down left in front of previous characters; DESIGNER and PRINTER enter from right and stand at down right in front of previous characters.)

REPORTER: I am a Reporter. I ask people questions about the event, and I do my own research to find additional facts. Then I turn over my information to the Editor.

EDITOR: I take the Reporter's information and shape it into an article or — in radio and television — a news segment. Then the article goes to a Designer.

DESIGNER: I take the article from the Editor and place it in the newspaper. I decide how big the type should be and choose a photo or picture. I decide on what page the article should appear and where it should appear on the page. Then I give the pages to the Printer. In radio and television, I am called a Director, and I choose when the news segments appear and in what order.

PRINTER: When the articles are ready to be printed and the news segments are ready to be broadcast, you need someone to operate the equipment. In newspaper publishing, I am called a Printer. In radio and television, I am called an Engineer.

ERIKA: How is information gathered? What are some of the tools a Reporter uses?

(Gary wheels the cart at mid center to down center and removes sheet to reveal news gathering items; Reporter, Editor, Designer and Printer cross to cart.)

REPORTER: *(holds up notepad and pen)* Every Reporter, whether they work for a newspaper or magazine, or a radio or television station, always carries a notepad and a pen or pencil. You use these tools to write down what you see and what people tell you about an event.

EDITOR: *(holds up micro-cassette recorder)* A Reporter also frequently uses an audio cassette recorder to record the sounds of an event and the exact words people say.

DESIGNER: *(holds up photo camera)* Many Reporters use a camera to take pictures of the event.

PRINTER: *(holds up video camera)* Or they use a video camera to record the sounds and pictures of the event as it happens.

REPORTER: Sometimes the Reporter is far away from the newspaper or station and has to send information about the event to the Editor. You can use a telephone *(holds up cell telephone)* and tell the information to the Editor.

EDITOR: *(holds up laptop computer)* Or, the Reporter can use a computer with a modem to send the information to a computer at the newspaper or station.

ERIKA: It sounds like there are many ways to gather and send information.

DESIGNER: There will be many more new ways in the years to come.

PRINTER: It wasn't long ago that machines like the telegraph and stock ticker were used to send information around the world. Now we have satellites in space that can send pictures from the far corners of our galaxy many light years away.

GARY: *(to audience)* Now it's your turn. Choose an event that has happened in your school or your town and decide how you would gather and publish the information.

ERIKA: *(to audience)* Remember, the best way to get information is to ask someone who knows. And that's our show for today.

GARY: Thanks for watching.

ERIKA: This has been Erika B.—
GARY: And Gary G.—
ERIKA: Reporters-at-large—
GARY: Signing off!

(LIGHTS OUT)

THE END

L.E. McCULLOUGH, PH.D. is an educator, playwright, composer and ethnomusicologist whose studies in music and folklore have spanned cultures throughout the world. Dr. McCullough is the Administrative Director of the Humanities Theatre Group at Indiana University-Purdue University at Indianapolis. Winner of the 1995 Emerging Playwright Award for his stage play *Blues for Miss Buttercup*, he is the author of *The Complete Irish Tinwhistle Tutor, Favorite Irish Session Tunes* and *St. Patrick Was a Cajun*, three highly acclaimed music instruction books, and has performed on the soundtracks for the PBS specials *The West, Lewis and Clark* and *Not for Ourselves Alone: The Story of Elizabeth Cady Stanton and Susan B. Anthony.* Since 1991 Dr. McCullough has received 43 awards in 31 national literary competitions and had 178 poem and short story publications in 90 North American literary journals. He is a member of The Dramatists Guild, American Conference for Irish Studies, Southeastern Theatre Conference and National Middle School Association. His books for Smith and Kraus include: *Plays of the Songs of Christmas; Stories of the Songs of Christmas; Ice Babies in Oz: Original Character Monologues; Plays of America from American Folklore, Vol. 1 & 2; Plays of the Wild West, Vol. 1 & 2; Plays from Fairy Tales; Plays from Mythology; Plays of People at Work; Plays of Exploration and Discovery; Anyone Can Produce Plays with Kids; Plays of Ancient Israel; Plays of Israel Reborn; 111 One-Minute Monologues for Teens, Vol. 2;* and *"Now I Get It!": 12 Ten-Minute Classroom Drama Skits for Elementary Science, Math, Language & Social Studies, Vol. 1 & 2.*